T0090525

Business After God's Heart

The Psalms of David Applied to the Heart of the Business Leader

WILLIAM PARKER

WESTBOW
PRESS®
A DIVISION OF THOMAS NELSON
& ZONDERVAN

WestBow Press books may be ordered through booksellers or by contacting:

WestBow Press
A Division of Thomas Nelson & Zondervan
1663 Liberty Drive
Bloomington, IN 47403
www.westbowpress.com
844-714-3454

Cover Design: Rachel G. Parker
Editor: Breana P. Parker

ISBN: 979-8-3850-1389-0 (sc)
ISBN: 979-8-3850-1391-3 (hc)
ISBN: 979-8-3850-1390-6 (e)

Library of Congress Control Number: 2023923093

Print information available on the last page.

WestBow Press rev. date: 02/20/2024

CONTENTS

INTRODUCTION

Seeing King David's
Heart for Business

Thanksgiving Business

It was the day after Thanksgiving 1998. I took the day off to drive my family from our home in the Washington, DC, area to visit Thomas Jefferson's historic Monticello home outside Charlottesville, Virginia. At the time, I was CEO of a NASDAQ-traded Christian internet company. On the way, my CFO called my cell phone to tell me that our stock, languishing for months, had begun to rise.

I turned and told the family, and everyone cheered since our stock had become an item of daily prayer during our family devotional time. Most of our kids in the van had no idea what stock was, but they knew "up" was good and "down" was bad and prayed accordingly. More phone calls followed as the stock picked up internet speed that day. In 1998, there were no smartphones, so progressively members of my team called to keep me abreast of what was happening in the market. With each call I would update my band of little prayer warriors as our ride to Charlottesville turned into a great celebration.

My dear wife, Linda, sitting beside me in the van, turned to look at me with tears of elation in her eyes. Unlike the kids, she understood the risk we had taken seven months prior in giving up a great job as a high-tech executive and following God's lead to accept the position at this tiny internet startup. I had begun with a small staff of only fifteen people and a closet office; it had been really tough, with a lot of setbacks, and very little visibility. But everything changed that day with my family as we drove toward Monticello. Linda saw, as I did, our vision for using the gifts God had given me to impact His kingdom beginning to be fulfilled.

Earlier that morning our internet community site had launched a Christian investment channel designed to inform believers about their investments related to social issues that were relevant to a Christian worldview. This awakened the broader investment community to what we were all about, which we desperately needed in order to raise the capital required to fulfill our mission. This was a huge breakthrough, even bigger than just the run on the stock. We were thankful it was a slow news day and a shortened trading day, because within half the day our company had quadrupled in value!

The calls continued to come, and we continued our rolling pep rally of excitement and praise on the way to Monticello. Soon enough my cell phone ran out of battery. Arriving at Monticello, I jumped out of our van and ran to find a public phone in the visitors center. While the family took their tour that day, I stood on the payphone fielding calls from the *Washington Post,* the local Washington TV news outlet, *CBS Market Watch,* and even CNBC. As I talked with CNBC, helping them understand who our company was and what we were trying to accomplish, I wondered, *Is this really happening?* When the family returned to the visitors center that afternoon, I told them I had just booked my first appearance on CNBC. Sensing my elation, the kids spontaneously cheered! And then they asked, "What is CNBC?"

What an amazing way to wrap up our family celebration of Thanksgiving that year! The ride home was filled with thankfulness to God for answered prayer and for His incredibly abundant provision to our family and the ministry business He had led Linda and me to pursue.

Heart Problems and King David

Barely more than a year later, my dear wife, who had celebrated with me in that van ride to Monticello, was sitting next to me in the hospital. I had started having periodic chest pains, and they reached a peak one evening in January 2000.

A month prior, I had begun to see problems with the business accumulate, many of which were my own doing, and a weakening market for our company. Stress reached extremely high levels. I found myself almost paralyzed by sleep deprivation and an overwhelming responsibility to the people, the business, and the ministry. In January 2000, after agonizing for weeks, I had gone to my board of directors with a plan to drastically cut the staff in an attempt to dive toward a sustainable business that wasn't dependent on the internet economy's craziness. This plan totally abandoned the strategy I had embarked the company on in early 1998. And with this plan, I knew we were approaching the end of my vision for this company.

During that December and January, I found myself weeping alone, or shouting out in anguish, over the reality of my miserable failure. Stress, depression, and insomnia gripped me. Over the course of fourteen months, I had gone from hotshot Christian business executive to business failure. Mentionings by Tom Brokaw on *NBC Nightly News,* feature articles in *USA Today* and *CBS Market Watch,* and multiple CNBC appearances were all long gone. Excitement about working with vaunted Christian ministry leaders, publishers, and musicians was forgotten.

I was sitting in the hospital emergency room that night, not knowing if I was having a heart attack and perhaps even on death's doorstep, when I reached the end of myself. In the season of brokenness and rebuilding that followed, I found myself going to the psalms again and again for solace and comfort. And there I found the heart of King David.

Brokenness to Breakthrough

> God raised up David to be their king, concerning whom
> He also testified and said, "I have found David the son
> of Jesse, a man after My heart, who will do all My will."
> From the descendants of this man, according to promise,
> God has brought to Israel a Savior, Jesus. (Acts 13:22–23)

Indeed, David was *a man after God's heart.* God looked at David's heart from the very beginning, when Samuel was led by God to select a new king to replace Saul. Samuel looked at the appearance of the sons of Jesse in selecting a king, but God looked at the heart (1 Samuel 16:7). He led Samuel to select David based on David's heart rather than his stature, his age, or his accomplishments.

I knew King David was not a perfect man. Yes, he conquered a giant and the Promised Land, but he also made giant mistakes and his sins were thorough in scope and depth. I could identify with David, not only because I shared some of the challenges he faced in rising to leadership and in leading each day but also because he, like me, was very far from perfect. But the amazing thing about this great leader was, despite all this, in Acts 13 he is still called "a man after God's heart."

The Business Breakthrough You Really Need from King David

Many of David's inspired psalms resonated with me deeply. As I poured over the book of Psalms, I really came to see and understand David's heart. In the psalms I saw both the elation and the agony of a heart that lived the triumphs and also lived the defeats on both a personal and corporate level. I certainly identified with this.

When I went to the Word of God for help in recovering personally from my devastating business failure, I recognized that God didn't give me a *Bible Manual for Business Leadership.* Rather, it became evident that God worked through me in business as an outflow of my heart-to-heart relationship with Him. I learned there is nothing more important in business leadership than walking through each business day, moment by moment, in the presence of almighty God. I began to see He really does have a relationship for me rather than a Christian business guide. And He gave me His own heart as my guide to this relationship. As His heart is reflected in my heart, the outflow of my heart in business reflects His heart in my business. As we read in Matthew 12:34–35, "For the mouth speaks of that which fills the heart. A good man brings good things out of the good stored up in him." This is the business breakthrough I truly needed!

Sun Tzu or King David

Countless books today offer practical help for the business leader. While useful, it seems reading a number of these books leaves you wondering whether you should develop habits or kick the habit, be a "one-minute manager" or look for "halftime," be "in search of excellence" or "manage by walking around." Maybe you should develop the habit of walking around in search of excellence because you only have one minute until halftime!

As I mined deeper into the psalms, it became apparent that David was relevant; while I might have once said, "David was no business leader," I began to see his similarities to my professional situations. David was a gifted strategist and tactician within his roles as warrior and king. Strategy and tactics were exactly where God had blessed me with gifts specific to business. From his youth, David progressively led larger forces until ultimately, as king, he was the commander in chief of the army of God in Israel and one of the greatest military minds of all time. David's tactics and strategies were guided and used by God to defeat all Israel's enemies and secure the Promised Land of Israel.

Many business leaders today apply the principles of the ancient Chinese general Sun Tzu from *The Art of War* to their business. In fact, legions of Sun Tzu devotees exist out there, applying the brilliance of a pagan conqueror to attack the marketplace for personal gain. How much better, I asked myself, to consider the brilliance of God's conqueror King David, a man after His own heart? Furthermore, the psalms continue to be "living and active" (Hebrews 4:12) as they are indeed part of the living and active Word of God for you and me today. No followers of Sun Tzu would dare to make such an amazing claim.

I also saw the similarities between David ruling over the kingdom of Israel and my role as a business leader "governing" over the work lives of my employees. Business leaders affect every aspect of their employees' work lives (and subsequently much of their personal lives too). They impact everything from deciding the work environment and everyday business processes to health care and compensation. As 2 Samuel 3:36 tells us, David was a loved and followed leader. The book of 1 Chronicles records David's considerable gifts as ruler: his organizational, managerial, and administrative skills for fiscal accountability; his delegation of authority; his identification and development of leadership; provision of emotional support; his establishment of extensive systems of local administration; and his practical leadership of the nation of God.

In the psalms we see that King David recognized his greatness, as an imperfect ruler over an imperfect people, was only a result of God's blessing in his life. And God blessed the people of Israel through King David. As a business leader, I wanted to see God's blessing in my life and in my business. I wanted to see God use me to bless my employees. So I decided that the heart of David would serve as my example.

The book you're holding reflects more than twenty years of meditation on this heart after God's heart. It began in a difficult season of my life and continued through years of learning, applying, relearning, and refining—all in the midst of leading six technology companies and strategically consulting owners of seven further companies. It may have begun in a season of reflection, meditation, and focused prayer, but it has been tested and refined in the day-to-day challenges of leading businesses for over two decades.

Beginning with a Prayer for You

Business after God's Heart is a challenge to the heart of the business leader to follow the heart of God as it's revealed in David's psalms. My prayer is that as your engagement in business flows from your heart, the resulting fruit of your heart will yield a business after God's heart. I'll begin by praying for you now and I suggest we pray with David's words from the beginning of Psalm 20, David's inspired prayer that he asked the Israelites to pray for him when he departed to lead his army into battle. "May the LORD answer you in the day of trouble! May the name of the God of Jacob set you securely on high! May He send you help from the sanctuary and support you from Zion!" Whether you are in a day of business trouble or not, my prayer is that God uses the lessons He has taught me to make you secure, send you help, and support you from His heavenly throne. Amen.

CHAPTER 1

One Thing

One thing I have asked from the Lord,
that I shall seek: that I may dwell in
the house of the Lord all the days of
my life, to behold the beauty of the
Lord and to meditate in His temple.
—Psalm 27:4

One Thing for Business Leadership Guidance and Power

David sought one thing: to spend each day in the presence of the almighty God of the universe. When you think about it, doing business in the very presence of almighty God would be the kind of thing that Indiana Jones would heroically spend his life pursuing. It connects the business leader to power and guidance. It transcends business and influences every area of life. No wonder David sought this. King David sought the edge—the secret, if you will—to practical power and guidance for enormous impact. And he had it.

So can you. Seeking this one thing is at the core of the heart after God's heart, and it's at the core of a heart that would have business after God's heart. Whatever we are facing in business must come after this heart desire to dwell in the presence of almighty God. Before business begins, our hearts seek one thing. "That I may dwell in the house of the Lord ... to behold His beauty and to meditate in His temple" (Psalm 27:4). After this one thing, business flows!

If any business leader should have had this experience, it should have been me. After all, I was CEO of a Christian business. But I missed it. And you may be missing it as well. I only discovered the opportunity and blessing of seeking the one thing that David sought in business as the Holy Spirit took me to the life of David, and this was ironically *after* I left the Christian business and began to engage in many other secular businesses. I saw how this great business leader led his enterprise while very practically living in the presence of God almighty; seeing this has had the greatest impact in my business life.

I knew when I stood in church that it was a good thing to seek God's presence and behold His beauty. However, when Monday morning rolled around and I was ordering my business day, consciously seeking and practically enjoying God's presence were far from my mind. Maybe I even had a great devotional time, which was very important to me, but when I fully turned my attention to business, I incredibly and tragically forfeited the opportunity—the gift—of doing business in the conscious presence of almighty God.

Perhaps it was my upbringing, perhaps I didn't see any examples, perhaps it was my self-reliance, perhaps it was my association, or perhaps I just considered the business world to be a totally different world. Church and devotions were great refreshment for my soul, but now it was time to get down to business. To be clear, I did seek to apply biblical principles to my business, and most of the time I followed through. After all, my life really was dedicated to God, and I was even an elder in my church. But in business I had objectives to accomplish and another way of thinking to go with it. I associated with a totally different crowd, applied different principles, and had different goals, and it was all business. The weekend or early morning break was over, and now I was exposed to serious stresses—and I would begin to operate on a totally different plane.

Although I did not consciously acknowledge this, in my heart of hearts, I decided to get back to devotion to God later since I had business to tend to right now. And off I went. By being double-minded instead of focusing on the one thing, I stepped out of the pathway of God's blessing. God had something better for me than that.

Can This Really Happen?

Maybe you can relate. Or you may be thinking that doing business in the very presence of God is an interesting thing to desire, and maybe it could happen in a spiritual realm beyond your awareness, but it's not something that could consciously influence your business day.

Perhaps your business life is filled with stresses and pressures, similar to one of my current client's situations. His business is going through the process of becoming a publicly traded company listed on the NASDAQ stock exchange. And since I was retained as a consultant to update the company's strategic plan but was not a principal in this case, I had the opportunity to observe the proceedings and interactions a bit more objectively.

Fur is flying! Wall Street analysts are going through the initial public offering; they visit the company, listen to presentations, and ask probing questions, all in an effort to place a value on the stock. The CEO, in preparation for going public, has recently shifted his strategy in order to take advantage of market opportunity and create better value. Consequently, the cofounder and number two man in the company has lost most of his resources and prestige. On top of this, a third principal has been promoted to chief operating officer (COO) of the company, receiving most of the company's resources and a new position of power—all but eclipsing the cofounder. Finally, the Wall Street analysts have overwhelmed the chief financial officer (CFO) with their need to understand financial performance and expectations, as the CFO simultaneously faces the difficult task of integrating finances of previously acquired companies.

This is a high-pressure, modern-day, and fairly common business situation. Great wealth, personal pride, and prestige are at stake. Offenses are taken. Past offenses are remembered. Tempers are flaring. Voices are raised. Is there really room *here* for "dwelling in the house of the Lord"?

David Also Had "Business" to Tend To

If we examine the context of Psalm 27:4, we realize it was not written from the mountaintop. Verse 2 reveals that David had some serious, pressing business to tend to. "When evildoers came upon me to devour my flesh, my adversaries and my enemies, they stumbled and fell." David was engaged in very serious "business" requiring his attention and the application of his skills and gifts. He was not in church. He had adversaries and enemies that were upon him. His troubles were so intense and personal that the image communicated is of adversaries seeking to devour his flesh. This is not just people who had it in for him in the business world. The adrenaline was pumping. They were seeking his life.

"Though a host encamp against me, my heart will not fear; though war arise against me, in spite of this I shall be confident" (Psalm 27:3). Here David makes it clear that the threat went beyond his personal safety. The safety and security of the whole nation were at stake. David and the people he was called to lead were being assaulted. Armies were camped around him, laying siege and planning their next move as they organized their deadly campaign. In the midst of this, David must plan his defense. He must think of tactics, consider the morale of his troops, and plan the logistics and positioning of his forces. David had to gather intelligence as well as be concerned about the enemy gathering intelligence from within his ranks.

David had world-class problems. The kind of predicament outlined in Psalm 27 is so extreme that few of us can readily identify with it. Yet it is from this place of tremendous "business" difficulties and stress that David says there is only one thing that he is seeking. What we see here from David is not just "Sunday school talk" but the expression of a heart that is being gravely tested. He was a real person like you, called to leadership by God, and gifted by God to do His will. David actually lived this. Identify with him. If David could seek God's presence continually, in the midst of real "business" life, then you can too!

Coming into His Presence for the First Time

God provided Jesus for you right where you are so that you can come into His presence in the next moment. You don't have to try to act religious or even make yourself better in any way. The first step to moving into the presence of God is one that involves a certain humility that may be foreign to the experience of many business leaders: we must be honest and acknowledge the sin that is in each of our lives. Deep inside, all of us know that we sin, but for many high-achieving business leaders, admitting to frailty can be a foreign concept. Romans 3:23 confirms what we know deep inside about ourselves, as it tells us that "all have sinned and fall short of the glory of God." All means *all;* that includes you and me. First John 1:8 says, "If we say we have no sin, we are deceiving ourselves and the truth is not in us." If we want to do business in the presence of almighty God, as David did, we must first acknowledge our sin and recognize also that Romans 6:23 tells us that the consequence of sin is spiritual death found in hell, as we are eternally separated from God.

"But God demonstrates His love for us in that while we were yet sinners, Christ died for us" (Romans 5:8). Through Christ, God provided a payment for our sins, so that we do not have to bear our punishment for them in hell. The perfect, sinless Son of God died as your substitute, paying the penalty for your sins. "He made Him who knew no sin to be sin on our behalf, so that we might become the righteousness of God in Him" (2 Corinthians 5:21). Receiving Christ's payment for your sins also means that you receive all of His righteousness so that you are given access to the very presence of holy God, now and for all eternity in heaven.

Jesus did this for all people, yet only those who receive this gift for themselves personally can experience His salvation from their sins. We're told very plainly in John 1:12, "But as many as received Him, to them He gave the right to become children of God, even to those who believe in His name." There must be a conscious decision to "receive" by faith God's gift of forgiveness and cleansing from sin, so freely available to you through Christ's sacrificial work on the cross.

Talking to God in a simple prayer is how you can verbalize your faith as you make that conscious decision to God. The specific words you say to God are not that important. He sees the sincerity and intent of your heart, regardless of what words are used.

If you just expressed your faith in prayer, you should praise God! The Bible tells us that there is great rejoicing in heaven going on right now (Luke 15:7). And you should be rejoicing too! You have just entered into the presence of God for the first time (believe it!), and you can live in His presence the rest of your life and for all eternity! This changes everything. This will revolutionize every aspect of your life, including your business life.

At this point, everyone reading should have had the opportunity to come into God's presence at least once, when they were saved. Perhaps many remember their salvation experience as a high point in their spiritual life to which they have never really returned. If so, the joy and peace experienced at salvation have been replaced by anxieties and the concerns of life at home and work. There have been trials, disappointments, and failures. There is much business to tend to and the stress of a busy schedule.

In this context, let's get back to David, a man after God's heart. As we've already discussed, David had tremendous trials in his life, yet the one thing that he continued to seek in the midst of these trials was to be in God's presence. Let's look at how we follow his example, seeking God's presence continually, even in our work environments.

The Powerhouse Position of Doing Business in the Presence of God

You may still be convinced that this just would not pan out in real life. However, living your business day in the conscious presence of almighty God—with His power, peace, joy, guidance, and confidence—is exactly what Jesus came to freely give! This is the very exciting and practical core principle to *Business after God's Heart*. It is not a magic formula for business success but rather the reason that Christ lived, died, and rose again. And as it is applied to your heart, it supernaturally impacts every aspect of your business.

We know from the New Testament that God no longer uniquely dwells in a certain physical temple. Rather, as 1 Corinthians 3:16 teaches, for the believer who has trusted Christ as Savior, his or her body is the very temple of God. "Do you not know that you are a temple of God and that the Spirit of God dwells in you?" And if God's Spirit dwells in us, then it stands to reason that we can spiritually dwell, or live, in the presence of God, just as David sought to do.

I am convinced the vast majority of good churchgoing Christian businesspeople seldom, if ever, practically experience life in the conscious presence of God. The reason for this dearth of experience may be explained in 1 John 1:5, "God is Light, and in Him there is no darkness at all." *Darkness* here equates to sin.

While the Spirit of God dwells in us, sin breaks fellowship with Him for in Him there is no darkness at all. Only those who are pure and holy can really experience the presence and active engagement with holy God. This standard is so high that if it is understood, many of us would immediately chalk it off as a practical impossibility and dismiss further consideration. Or maybe we rationalize our behavior, not recognizing the sin in our own hearts, living as if all is OK. In either scenario, however, we are living outside God's practical engagement in our lives. We are living beyond the reach of His very real and accessible power and guidance for each business day.

The next verse in 1 John goes on to caution us—believers—to not kid ourselves about this. "If we say that we have fellowship with Him and yet walk in darkness, we lie and do not practice the truth." The experience of the presence and fellowship with God can be very real in our business lives, *yet we cannot experience His fellowship if there is any sin in our lives*. Of course, none of us are perfect so this paradox can only be resolved by our perfect Creator as we are perfectly forgiven and restored. In doing that God offers us this amazing opportunity to do business in His very presence with His active engagement! Praise Him! This powerhouse position changes everything in life and business.

How to Practice Business in His Presence

David said that the one thing he sought was to "dwell in the house of the Lord" in the midst of all his challenges. The Spirit paints a clear and vivid picture of the opportunity we have to personally and practically experience business in the presence of God in Hebrews 10:19–22.

> Therefore, brethren, since we have confidence to enter the holy place by the blood of Jesus, by a new living way which He inaugurated for us through the veil, that is, His flesh ... let us draw near with a sincere heart in full assurance of faith, having our hearts sprinkled clean from an evil conscience and our bodies washed with pure water.

God, through Christ, makes dwelling in His presence a practical reality. It's right there in front of us. It's up to us to humbly seek that one thing that David sought. This powerhouse position of faith can be ours to the extent that we make our faith practical in the day-to-day routine of business leadership. Let's talk about how this can be our experience.

1. Examine your heart, guard your heart, and be honest about sin.

Remember 1 John 1:5 tells us that "God is Light, and in Him there is no darkness at all." There is no darkness—*no sin*—in Him. We can't harbor darkness or sin we know we have in our heart and at the same time enjoy the fellowship with God. The core reason Christian business leaders are not doing their business in the conscious presence of almighty God, as David sought to do, is because of sin in their lives.

I'm not talking about robbing a convenience store kind of sin or making false statements to the Securities and Exchange Commission, but sin just the same. Any sin. Any sin in our thoughts is a sin that breaks our fellowship with God.

Even though we have received Christ as our Savior, we must continue to allow Him to purify our hearts. For very successful people this kind of humility about our thought life can be tough. If we are not honest about the sins of the heart, however, we forfeit the opportunity that Christ came to give: experiencing life and business in the conscious presence of almighty God. Very similar to our salvation experience, we acknowledge our sin so that we can allow God to remove our sin. Colossians 2:6 strongly reinforces the similarity of our daily experience with our salvation experience. "Therefore as you have received Christ Jesus the Lord, so walk in Him."

When we first came to Christ, we knew we were sinners completely dependent on His grace for salvation and cleansing. After we've been Christians for a while, we begin to trust in our own "righteousness" rather than being humbly dependent only on Christ to make us holy. Then when our efforts fall short, we can tend to rationalize, justify, or deny our thoughts and behavior, but this prevents us from living in a place of actively enjoying the presence of God! We are called to simply come back to Christ for forgiveness and cleansing, in complete humility, very similar to the way we did when we were saved.

2. As you confess your sin, be certain that you have been forgiven based on the authority of God's Word, totally cleansed, and made holy.

"If we confess our sins, He is faithful and righteous to forgive us our sins and to cleanse us from *all* unrighteousness" (1 John 1:9; emphasis mine). Jesus Christ was offered to pay for your sin. The payment is sufficient and because of that, "there is no longer any offering for sin" (Hebrews 10:18). Incredible as it sounds, and contrary to the views of many religious folks, there is nothing more you must do to be cleansed and made completely pure and directly engaged with our holy God. Believe it! Be certain of His complete cleansing. Enjoy this purity that He gives. Real faith in the effectiveness of Christ's blood to completely cleanse transforms the way you feel. What a powerful mindset for leadership. This powerful, guilt-free mindset is not because of anything you've done or failed to do. It's just and only because of the effectiveness of the blood of Christ applied to your heart.

3. Follow David to experience the one thing he sought, as you come confidently into the presence of holy God.

By faith, make this experience of Hebrews 10:19–22 certain very practically in the middle of your business day. That is, respond to the exhortation of the Spirit, through the provision of Christ's work, and by faith *confidently* "enter the holy place by the blood of Jesus, by a new living way which He inaugurated for us through the veil, that is, His flesh ... let us draw near with a sincere heart in full assurance of faith, having our hearts sprinkled clean from an evil conscience and our bodies washed with pure water." Spiritual confidence is just plain confidence, and it will manifest in the trials and opportunities of business just as it did for David as he said, "Though a host encamp against me, my heart will not fear; though war arise against me, in spite of this I shall be confident" (Psalm 27:3).

Our practical confidence comes to life even more as we understand that in referring to the "holy place" (Hebrews 10:19), the Spirit takes us back to the image of the Old Testament temple that David alluded to in Psalm 27. The holy place is the place of the presence of God—the place where David sought to be. Because Jesus's blood paid the price for your sin *and made you holy,* you can enter the holy place of God's presence. This verse tells you that you should enter into His presence *confidently.* This confidence is not because of anything that you have done or avoided doing, but your confidence is in the blood of Jesus to pay for your sin and make you holy. As you've asked the Lord to examine your heart, and you've honestly confessed and turned from any sin that He reveals, confidently enter the holy place of His presence!

Implicit in all of this is faith. We are challenged to the faith of King David and exhorted to "draw near [to God almighty] … in full assurance of faith." Hebrews 11:1 gives us the closest thing to a dictionary definition of faith we see on any word in the Bible. "Now faith is the assurance of things hoped for, the conviction of things not seen."

Focusing just on "the assurance of things hoped for," we can understand that faith is the firm persuasion and certain expectation that God will perform all that He has promised. So we draw near to God as David did, totally persuaded and certain that God has cleansed us and invited us into His presence at the moment we receive His forgiveness. This persuasion is so strong that at the beginning of our thoughts, senses, and emotions (in our soul), it really has happened. It is reality. Our perfect cleansing and our presence with God almighty are the certain realities that our thoughts, senses, and emotions recognize.

Faith is also "the conviction of things not seen." Forgiveness, spiritual cleansing, and the presence of God are things that can't be seen. Faith registers to the mind the firm reality of these things promised by God even though they can't be seen. These faith images are placed in the mind at the same place that sight images are placed in the mind. By making real to the mind these things that can't be seen, faith motivates us to actions that are consistent with the nature and importance of this faith. This kind of faith gives us the tangible confidence that King David had to consciously enter the presence of the God of the universe!

This is to be our practical experience in business. This is not some kind of mind game, but it is the reason that God sent Jesus to die for us. He wants us to do business very practically in His presence, receiving His strength, guidance, and blessing. What a powerful position to lead from! This one thing is exactly what David sought, and through Christ it is available to you and me.

4. Use faith triggers to practice seeking God's presence.

We have all developed patterns and habits that may not change easily. For all your business life you've engaged in routines that will not necessarily prompt you to consciously seek the presence of God through the course of your day. Recognizing this. I've found that it's helpful to develop some "faith triggers" to help me follow the heart of David through my business day.

Faith triggers are physical cues that prompt me to exercise my faith in seeking to consciously experience His presence during my daily routine. For example, a couple of my faith triggers are any time I walk into a conference room, or whenever I go to the office kitchen for coffee. When you come across one of your faith triggers, quickly examine your heart, and in a moment confess any sin He reveals (maybe just an attitude, a lack of faith or an un-loving thought), and then exercise your real faith in God's perfect cleansing, your position in His presence—and enjoy it! This is not stopping everything, bowing your head, and spending focused time in prayer. It's just a moment of purposeful reflection. It's a quick *bang, bang, bang* as you walk down the hall or sit in your chair. With your eyes wide open, you can see that you have just moved with confidence into the very presence of almighty God and He will change your countenance and give you exactly what you need for the next moment.

The best faith triggers are the ones that you define from your own environment, so select some that will be helpful for you. For example, when I walk into a conference room, I'm conscious of it. There is usually some kind of business challenge that will be addressed in the near future and that challenge will be addressed with other colleagues. So when I walk into a conference room, I walk in the conscious awareness of the presence of almighty God! He's there for me, and I have real confidence in Him for that meeting. Entering the office kitchen for coffee is something that I make a conscious decision to do. When I make that decision and start for the kitchen, this faith trigger prompts me to be in God's presence as I go and possibly interact with people. If I'm in God's presence during such kitchen-and-hallway-encounters with folks, then they will be interacting with someone who—from God's presence—can really touch their lives with His power.

Other faith triggers may be when you go to your boss's office, when a subordinate comes to your office, when you open a certain software application, when you check your smartphone, when you put on your helmet to walk a job site, when you fasten your seatbelt on the way to work, or when you greet the receptionist or the gate guard. You get the idea. Applying these faith triggers will be a real help as you seek to do business in the conscious presence of God. They practically interrupt thought patterns and routines that you have formed over the years.

You don't have to read the rest of this book to begin applying this. You can begin right now by defining your faith triggers. And you can spend your next business day largely in the conscious awareness of the presence of God! The heart after God's heart *seeks* to be there.

Seeking the One Thing Is Very Practical

Hopefully, you're seeing how this becomes very practical in your business day. Knowing what's available to you, however, does not make the experience automatic. In fact, although David said that he sought to dwell in the house of the Lord, the Bible does not indicate he was always there. The reality is he couldn't possibly be, and understanding the life of David, we know for sure he was not always there. Yet in the book of Acts, the Spirit tells us long after David's death that David did have the heart after God's heart. And the heart after God's heart *seeks* to experience God's presence. Like David, you will not always be there either, but like David, you can seek to be there.

Even this morning, as I write this, I know I will face the pressures today of a very important meeting. I have the opportunity to stand up in front of a large New York private equity company and brief a business plan for combining several companies into one, creating critical mass and a strong competitor in its market. Today, I will finish the preparation and then interact for about two hours in an attempt to communicate and persuade. This is a tremendous opportunity.

My temptation will be to focus on everything associated with the meeting and not seek the one thing that really matters. If I focus just on the meeting, success and failure, others' perception of me or the business concept, instead of first seeking to experience God's presence and then continuing to seek His presence, I lose. I lose His peace, His joy, His perspective, and His confidence. Instead of this meeting being about Him, at the core of it, it becomes about me. And I have subtly shifted from a position of real dependence on the God of the universe to dependence on myself. While I am really depending on myself, I may perhaps make a request for God to bless my activities. God wants me to seek the one thing that matters: His presence. It's all about Him. This business is to be about His glory, not mine.

If I approach this business today truly seeking one thing, then He will get the glory and my praise. And as He lifts my head up, I do want to praise Him, just as I see from Psalm 27:6 when David says, "I will sing, yes, I will sing praises to the Lord." If my heart is right, the rest will flow. I don't need a bunch of Christian business commandments. I need a heart that's right—a heart after God's heart. And He will guide and lead as I confidently depend on Him.

The Business Breakthrough for You

Doing business in the presence of almighty God, like King David, is the incredible business breakthrough available to you today. God offers *you* His presence, just as He did David. The thought of living the rest of your life consciously in the very presence of God may seem a little overwhelming. However, the thought of exercising faith to spend the next moment consciously experiencing His presence does not seem so overwhelming. You can take a step in a moment, and then take another step in the next moment. You don't have to take on the rest of your life in this moment, or even the rest of the day; you only have to apply faith to the next moment.

As you continue to apply faith moment by moment, before you know it, you are "dwelling" in the conscious presence of God. By applying faith like this, you have the opportunity to do business in the presence of the God of the universe, on a very practical basis. As you live this way, moment by moment, you begin to understand what a business life of faith really is on an everyday level.

This is the first and most important principle to *Business after God's Heart*. From here you are in position to receive God's wisdom, guidance, and comfort to lead in business tactics and strategies and to oversee those entrusted to your management and care. Doing business in the conscious presence of the almighty God of the universe is the key to this. No wonder David said this is the one thing that he shall seek. What an awesome opportunity is available to you and me as we lead in our businesses—and Christ paid a tremendous price so that this might be so.

CHAPTER 2

Business with a Clean Heart

Create in me a clean heart, O God,
and renew a steadfast spirit within me.
—Psalm 51:10

I'm No King David

At this point you may be thinking, *I'm no King David,* and you're right. You're thinking about what an extraordinary man of God he was, and although you have gifts and abilities that you apply to business, you're not even a pastor. You're a business leader! We've already established the similarity though of David's "business" with your own. And now we will look at the reality of David's frailty, and you will again identify with a great man of God—a man after God's heart—who was also a sinner like you and me.

My journey of recovery from business failure, and also the greatest time of spiritual growth in my life, really began in Psalm 51 with David and his need for God to give him a clean heart. I don't know about you, but it thrills my soul to know that this sinner knew he was made righteous by the grace of God alone. When I think about my life in business, I know there have been so many days that I have just lived in sin. I've been deceitful and unloving. Not even a moment of prayer. Not a moment to acknowledge God in any way. Certainly, no confession of sins committed, much less an awareness of the sins of my heart. I have lived this life of spiritual squalor at work, all the while coming home to lead my family spiritually and go to church on the weekends. Over time, this kind of living has had consequences in my business, in my family, in my church, and even in my physical body.

In David, God showed me another imperfect and failed heart that He completely restored! Not just restored but made completely righteous by His power, mercy, and grace. This overjoyed my soul! Despite all my sins and failures, God wanted to use me in business just as He used King David. As I imitated David's faith in God's power and grace to forgive me and make me completely righteous, I was practically moved by God to a position of stability and confidence that He paid such a dear price to provide. Despite my failures and my sins, He gave me a very happy place to operate from each day. Let's allow David, the heart after God's heart, to guide us all to this happy place of business leadership.

The Marvel of God's Grace and Mercy in David's Life

We will always be impressed with David's exploits—his great leadership, his abilities as a warrior, his wonderfully inspired poetry, and his sensitivity to the heart of God—but the most amazing thing about David is God's grace and mercy demonstrated in his life. David was a sinner … big time! He sinned in every area of his life. He sinned on such a large scale, and with such far-reaching consequences, that it's amazing God chose to place him in such a pivotal position in all time and eternity. The real marvel of David is the marvel of the grace and mercy of God in a life. Many of David's psalms marvel at this aspect of God's character as they express David's real heart. There is no way to study and apply this heart after God's heart without understanding the depth of David's sin.

David's Sin Started in His Business

Most are familiar with David's very famous failure: his sin of adultery with Bathsheba. Many might not recognize though this great personal, moral failure was actually set in motion by David's sin in his "business."

David was king of Israel. His business was the business of a king. His personal calling from God was clearly to conquer the Promised Land and secure it from all Israel's enemies. David had to engage personally, by using his God-given gifts and following God's guidance to lead strategically and tactically, to accomplish this calling.

Yet in 2 Samuel 11:1 we observe, "Then it happened in the spring, at the time when kings go out to battle, that David sent Joab and his servants with him and all Israel, and they destroyed the sons of Ammon and besieged Rabbah. But David stayed in Jerusalem." Here we see David did not take care of business. The job of the king is to go to war when the nation goes to war. David didn't. As a result of this disobedience, he is at home with time on his hands. He evidently uses this time to sleep the day away, as we see that he is rising from his bed when evening came. "Now when evening came David arose from his bed and walked around on the roof of the king's house … and from the roof he saw a woman bathing; and the woman was very beautiful in appearance" (2 Samuel 11:2). Observe the time that he took to himself instead of going to war was used to indulge in slothfulness and later lust. Then because David was not with his troops in the field, and Bathsheba's husband was, there was opportunity for the sin of lust to be acted upon.

David Doubles Down on Business Sins

After committing adultery, when David finds out that Bathsheba is pregnant, he immediately uses his power, influence, and reputation in his "business" in an attempt to obscure his sin.

> The woman conceived; and she sent and told David, and said, "I am pregnant." Then David sent to Joab [David's general], saying, "Send me Uriah the Hittite." So Joab sent Bathsheba's husband Uriah to David. When Uriah came to him, David asked concerning the welfare of Joab and the people and the state of the war. Then David said to Uriah, "Go down to your house, and wash your feet." (2 Samuel 11:5–8)

Using his "business" authority to cover his personal sin began with calling Bathsheba's husband, Uriah, back from the fight ostensibly to discuss the progress of the battle. In this account we see the progression of callousness of David's sins as he attempts to manipulate Uriah to go to his beautiful wife and make love to her so that David's sin might be covered. See how Uriah's righteousness thwarts David's plans when Uriah says to David, "'The ark and Israel and Judah are staying in temporary shelters, and my lord Joab and the servants of my lord are camping in the open field. Shall I then go to my house to eat and to drink and to lie with my wife? By your life and the life of your soul, I will not do this thing'" (2 Samuel 11:11).

Undeterred by Uriah's righteousness, David again uses his authority in his "business" to further sin, as he directs his general to deliberately have Uriah killed in battle so David can then take the widow as his wife. "Now in the morning David wrote a letter to Joab and sent it by the hand of Uriah. He had written in the letter, saying, 'Place Uriah in the front line of the fiercest battle and withdraw from him, so that he may be struck down and die'" (2 Samuel 11:14–15). David's personal sin results in directing Joab, his general, to use terrible tactics and to effectively commit murder, so that his personal sin might be covered.

These were not David's only sins by any means. He had other sins in both his personal and business life. The nest of sins associated with his adultery with Bathsheba, however, and the murder of Uriah provide a vivid, condensed look at the way David's sin moved from business to personal and back to business. This great man of God disobeyed God in "business," was slothful in business, lusted in his heart after a woman, committed adultery, abused his power in business to deceive, abused his power in business to murder, and finally took a righteous servant's wife.

From this we must recognize that sins in business cannot somehow be isolated to business. We must be pure in business or we're not pure at all. And the sins of business, if not dealt with, will lead us to sin in all areas of our lives.

David Had Reasons for Denial and So Do We

David certainly must have felt embarrassed. It probably contributed to the measures he took to cover his sin. He was the great king of Israel and he wisely judged and punished people for committing lesser sins than his own. People danced in the streets to celebrate his greatness when he returned from battle. What tremendous pressure he must have felt to keep silent about his sin. What great embarrassment he faced as he dealt with his sins. Some of us, like David, keep silent and deny our sin because we are too embarrassed to face it. When our business ascent has been great and public failure has been rare, we begin to believe the PR about our lives.

David's pride was the real source of his embarrassment. It blinded him to his need to turn humbly from his sin. In our culture today, pride in business is lifted as a virtue rather than a vice. Admitting mistakes is not generally considered a good way to get ahead. And confessing to "sins" is unheard of in the workplace. This pattern is firmly established from grade school to business school and has been reinforced ever since.

When this business culture of pride and deceit regarding our business behavior penetrates our psyche, it can be difficult to be honest with ourselves about the condition of our heart. This leads us to spiritual defeat and more sin rather than the restoration and cleansing that God offers. The self-deception will encumber our business effectiveness and inhibit the power God would provide as we are made holy by His grace and put in position to be led and blessed by Him.

David undoubtedly enjoyed his season of sin with Bathsheba. He was creating sinful methods to continue in it, rather than confess and forsake his sin. We too may continue to live in sin in business because we like it and even profit from it. As a result, we really don't want to give it up. For example, when we have been using a deceptive sales presentation to great effect, received commissions, and been publicly recognized for winning based on this deception, it can be tough to call sin "sin" and turn from it.

In reality, what we do in such situations is deny God. We deny His power to enable us to sell or otherwise succeed honestly. We prefer the deceitfulness of sin just as David did. And in that deceitfulness, we find a way to justify our actions and assuage our conscience. In doing so, we fail to step into the pathway of the blessing from the God of the universe, preferring instead to stay in sin and subject ourselves to its ultimate consequences.

For these reasons, and many others, it is often difficult to acknowledge sins in business, turn from them, and receive forgiveness and restoration from God. Even now you may be reacting to what you've read with more rationalization, more attempts to justify your sins, or more denial. In this regard, the heart of David gives us a very scary psalm. "If a man does not repent, [God] will sharpen His sword; He has bent His bow and made it ready. He has also prepared for Himself deadly weapons; He makes His arrows fiery shafts" (Psalm 7:12–13). We may not see the immediate impact of unrepentant sin in our life and business, as God allows time for repentance. However, God hates sin, He is just, and He speaks from the heart of David in Psalm 7 to make us understand that there ultimately will be consequences as He pursues us.

Judgment of David's Sin

Sadly, judgment came to David in the death of the son that Bathsheba conceived.

> Nathan said to David, "The LORD also has taken away your sin; you shall not die. However, because by this deed you have given occasion to the enemies of the LORD to blaspheme, the child also that is born to you shall surely die." (2 Samuel 12:13–14)

In addition, there was an extended period of time during David's denial of his sin that he was far from enjoying the presence of God. As we will see from Psalm 32, this time of separation had a great negative effect on David's life spiritually, psychologically, and even physically.

> When I kept silent about my sin, my body wasted away through my groaning all day long. For day and night Your hand was heavy upon me; my vitality was drained away as with the fever heat of summer. (Psalm 32:3–4)

We see here David's silence about his sin led to stress and anxiety. At some point this stress crosses over from the mental or emotional realm into the physical realm. These verses describe the effect of sin on David's whole person, including his body. The heavy hand of God, pressing down on his life day and night, left David in sleeplessness, weakness, and probably depression.

Business with a Stressful Heart

At this point, we pause to take a closer look at stress with the heart of David. He clearly had his times of stress, as all Christian business leaders do. I've certainly felt it. In fact, I came to accept stress as something that goes with a good, important job. I just thought it had to be part of business leadership and accepted it as a price I had to pay. King David's openness about his stress and its causes was a revelation to me as I dug deeper into his psalms. As a Christian, is it necessary for you and me to pay this price too? Before we conclude looking at David's sin and God's grace in his life, it is critical to understand where stress comes from and that there is no need for it to remain.

Caused by a Lack of Faith

We are commanded to walk by faith. Romans 14:23 says that "whatever is not from faith is sin." And we know from 1 John 3:1 that God loves you personally. "See how great a love the Father has bestowed on us, that we would be called children of God; and such we are."

You are to "walk" by faith in God's love for you. You are also to walk by faith in His sovereign power and goodness working on your behalf. A wonderful synopsis is found in Romans 8:28. "And we know that God causes all things to work together for good to those who love God, to those who are called according to His purpose."

Having said this, there is enormous uncertainty in business. And if you do not face this uncertainty with real faith in God's love for you as His dear child, and sovereign power and goodness working on your behalf, then this uncertainty will result in stress. The stress though is not ultimately caused by the uncertainty. The stress is caused by a lack of faith in God's love, power, sovereignty, and goodness. Stress and anxiety do not come from outside; rather, they are generated on the inside as a response to what's happening on the outside.

For example, there is no stress in watching a rerun of a football game. The action is all the same as when the game was originally played, but because you know the outcome, you don't experience the stress. In the same way, if you have faith in God's infinite love for you and His divine sovereignty in your life, then stress is removed even in the midst of temporal uncertainty. This is because you know the outcome, or in other words, you have faith.

As we consider our business challenges through the eyes of faith in God, stress goes away. As we enter an important meeting or compete for business really needed to sustain the business, while also having God's perspective, we will have faith in Him and be at peace.

What to Do When Stress Comes

Let's return to Romans 14:23. Since "whatever is not of faith is sin," the lack of faith, which caused the stress, must be confessed when it surfaces. And as you confess this sin, you pray for faith in His love, His power, and all of His attributes! This is a prayer that God wants to answer, and He does, when prayed from a heart that He just made pure. With the real faith that He provides comes real peace amid uncertainty. The alternative is to "manage" this "little sin" like most of us do and continue with stress rather than the peace that comes from real faith.

You may be thinking, *Whoa, Hoss! This standard is too high. I will be constantly going to God for forgiveness.* Good point. And what's the problem with that? How do you think a business leader becomes humble? Real humility comes as we are dependent on the God of the universe for a pure heart and everything else. You need not go through catastrophic failure to obtain this true humility.

Use Stress as a Barometer for Your Soul

Since stress can be an indication that sin has come into your life, it can be a great barometer for your soul in business. In the sailing days, the ship's captain was his own weatherman, and the barometer was his most important tool. The barometer told the captain that the weather conditions had changed before he could see the weather changing. When his survival may be dependent upon staying out of a storm, knowing this early is extremely important. With this knowledge, together with wind direction, he could position his ship to avoid the pending storm.

Stress can function for the business leader like the barometer for the ship's captain. It can tell us that sin has entered into our lives, perhaps subtly, before we have any other visible indication of trouble. Based on this indication of your "stress barometer," you can look at your life and ask the Lord to search your heart. Then as you confess your sin, you maneuver away from a coming storm of more and greater sin—and more severe consequences of said sin. Not only that, but as you are forgiven God, takes away the stress, changes your perspective, and creates a clean heart! This barometer can help keep you humbly dependent on God's grace and avoid the rough and damaging seas of further sin.

Denying Our Lack of Faith and the Other "Little" Sins

On the other hand, when we don't call the "little" sins of the heart "sins," the continuation in this sin will likely begin to mentally and physically affect us. David tells us what happened when he kept silent about his own sins (Psalm 32:3–4).

It's clear in our day and age that stress, oftentimes related to work, can lead to mental or emotional problems. It is no stretch for us to recognize that stress can lead to physical problems too. There is a clear connection between stress and heart disease, ulcers, and back problems, to name a few of the most obvious. David's account in Psalm 32 provides a good description of a person living in a lot of stress, with mental and physical consequences that occur over time. "My body wasted away through my groaning all day long … my vitality was drained away as with the fever heat of summer" (verses 3–4).

So just as our slide into sin begins with "little" things—like a lack of faith in almighty God and His infinite love for us—the physical consequences of our "little sins" begin with little things. Then the consequences get bigger as we continue in sin, unaware, in denial, in rationalization, or in justification. It begins with insomnia; it ends in depression. It begins with a stiff neck, and it ends with a slipped disk. It begins with an acid stomach, and it ends with an ulcer. It begins with worry and it ends with heart disease. It begins with the things we don't call sins. If we don't call them sins, and they are sins, then we are in denial and likely headed for much bigger storms in our life and business.

David says in Psalm 32 that he was severely stressed. David also says he received relief for this stress when he unloaded all his sin. The same relief available to David then is available to us now.

No Mess Is Too Big for God to Fix

As we've seen, David's "little" sins grew and led to huge sins in both his personal and business life. He made a big mess that impacted the people close to him and the people of an entire nation (everyone in his "business"). He made a mess, and he was a mess.

You have not made any worse messes than David made. You too can follow David's example (the example of the heart after God's heart) in allowing the Lord, by His grace, to forgive it all, and to completely restore your life. Let's look at David's recovery that he captured for us in Psalm 51.

> I know my transgressions and my sin is ever before me. Against You, You only, I have sinned and done what is evil in Your sight, so that You are justified when You speak and blameless when You judge … Purify me with hyssop, and I shall be clean; wash me, and I shall be whiter than snow. Make me to hear joy and gladness, let the bones which You have broken rejoice. Hide Your face from my sins and blot out all my iniquities. Create in me a clean heart, O God, and renew a steadfast spirit within me. (Psalm 51:3–4; 7–10)

Here David leads us to see that acknowledging our sin is the first step to allowing God, by His grace, to restore us. After that, we ask for His forgiveness and cleansing. And finally, we are to have faith in the effectiveness of His cleansing in our hearts. This very closely parallels the exhortation of 1 John 1:9. "If we confess our sins, He is faithful and righteous to forgive us our sins and to cleanse us from all unrighteousness."

Acknowledging Sin and Being Forgiven

As we saw in the last chapter, God wants to give you His grace and mercy rather than His judgment. Don't be confused by thinking that living in the house of the Lord, as David sought to do, is about your perfect performance. As it turns out, this one thing is based on God's grace and mercy. God wants to cleanse you completely and bless your life and your business, as only He can do. It's so simple, so thorough, and so liberating. Don't continue to live in the squalor of denial, rationalization, or justification as David did for a time. Follow this great man's example of coming out of it. Face your sin, as David faced his sin, be made pure and holy by God, and expect God's blessing in your life and business as He *completely* forgives your past sins.

David, the one who was called the man after God's heart, was not perfect by any means. Yet this ruined sinner stands in the line of Christ. This is amazing grace! Jesus Christ, who was called the Son of David, came to bring ruined sinners like David, you, and me into the presence of holy God. David, the man after God's heart, did not earn the blessing of God but received it as a gift of God's grace and mercy. David was made righteous by God. He prayed that God would create in him a clean heart, and God answered his prayer. It was this heart, created by God through His cleansing power, that was "after God's heart." It was *all* God's work in David's life.

Just as God created a clean heart for David, He sent the Son of David (Jesus Christ) to offer a clean heart to you and me. This should give you great hope and encouragement. Again, 1 John 1:9 says, "If we confess our sins, He is faithful and righteous to forgive us our sins and to cleanse us from all unrighteousness." All unrighteousness. Not some, *all*. We don't have to make ourselves clean. That's His job. We may be tempted to think that the sin is too great, or the combination of sins is too entangling. Look at David's failures and reject this deception. We may be tempted to be too proud or embarrassed to face them. Look at the life of one of the greatest leaders of all time; follow his example of going from humble confession to the true greatness that comes as a gift from God. We may be tempted to continue rationalizing sins in business because we like them and profit from them. Understand that these are very short-term returns, leading to certain immediate consequences and long-term ruin.

Righteous Business Leadership

Many of David's psalms are written from the point of view of the righteous one. We see this throughout most of his psalms, including in Psalm 18:20, where we read, "The LORD has rewarded me according to my righteousness; according to the cleanness of my hands He has recompensed me." Yet we know for certain that David was a gross sinner. And we also know that this sinner was in the line of Christ, and Christ Himself was called the Son of David. David had a faith in God's forgiveness and cleansing that made him really see himself as righteous.

God calls us to this kind of faith. God calls us to lead our business from a position of righteousness before God, because of the effectiveness of the blood of Jesus applied to our hearts. So as business leaders, let us embrace the spiritual power that comes from imitating David's faith in the perfect cleansing and resulting righteousness Christ offers. What a powerful position for your soul to rest in as you lead your business.

Happy Business Leadership

In Psalm 32:1 David says, "How blessed is he whose transgression is forgiven, whose sin is covered!" The word "blessed" can be translated for us as the word "happy." David is telling us that a forgiven business leader is a happy business leader. Businesses should be run by happy souls! Having been forgiven, David's condition is happy. His state of mind is happy. His prospects are happy currently, in the immediate future, and in the long-range future. This happiness is independent of the business plan, the profit and loss statement, the size of the bonus, or the project assigned.

The business leader is happy because it's a very happy thing to live in the presence of the God of the universe. It is a blessing to enjoy His infinite and unconditional love and to be certain of His care in the middle of each business day. And we can only get there by being forgiven.

God's exhortation through David to your heart is to be happy through His forgiveness as you lead your business.

> Make glad the soul of Your servant, for to You, O Lord, I lift up my soul. For You, Lord, are good, and ready to forgive, and abundant in lovingkindness to all who call upon You. (Psalm 86:4–5)

This truly is the happiness that's given by the grace of God.

It's also a happy thing to run a business without stress. It's a happy thing to work in a business where the boss is not stressed. It makes everyone happy. And when everyone is happy, the boss is even happier! Our religious performance will never take us there, nor will our own goodness or our own righteousness. Only by God's forgiveness, as we apply it to hearts, do we become *divinely happy* business leaders.

Business with a Clean Heart

It's God design for you, as a business leader, to operate with a perfectly pure heart that He creates, just as He did for King David. From here you are empowered by God to accomplish His purposes for you in business. From here you touch people and business with God's power. David (with the "clean heart" he prayed for at the beginning of Psalm 51) understands in Psalm 51:13 that this purity will lead to God's power and effectiveness. "Then I will teach transgressors Your ways, and sinners will be converted to You."

We certainly should understand very clearly from David's life that we don't get this pure heart by our perfect performance. It's only by the blood of Jesus applied to our hearts. What an encouragement this is to us, to know that the heart after God's heart was not perfect but perfectly forgiven. And because of God's perfect forgiveness, you and I can function like David did—empowered by God—for supernatural effectiveness.

CHAPTER 3

The Broken Business Leader

The sacrifices of God are a broken spirit;
a broken and a contrite heart, O God,
You will not despise. —Psalm 51:17

The Crucified CEO

No business book today suggests that the CEO should be broken. If there was a book today entitled *The Crucified CEO*, it might be purchased by an entirely different crowd. No course at any business school espouses brokenness as a principle of business leadership. Yet the "heart after God's heart," the heart of King David, was broken. In fact, the great warrior and ruler King David, chosen by God to secure the Promised Land and from whom would come the Messiah, said "I am a worm and not a man" (Psalm 22:6). This is hardly what we expect to hear from a business leader, much less one of the greatest leaders to ever live. Why is it that David can say this and we do not bring ourselves to say it?

When people talk about a "brokenness experience," they are usually referring to a bone-crushing blow to one's life so devastating it forces a reexamination of the very foundation life is built upon. However it comes, the effect often brings down the house of cards an individual has built around a reliance on self and forces them to rely only on the God of their salvation. God brought David to brokenness in this way, and He did so with me as well. In fact, this book you're holding was literally born out of my brokenness experience.

It's God's will that you learn brokenness from the Word of God and as the Word is made more real by the example of others (like David and maybe even me), rather than requiring God to permit your life to be devastated for you to live the broken life that God intends—so listen carefully.

Dot-Bomb Brokenness

By horrific business failure God taught me the deep lessons of brokenness and dependence upon Him. While God has blessed my life with business success, and used me to provide insights to folks who are building their businesses, it is through this brokenness that He gave me an even greater blessing that has touched every area of my life. You see, in 1998 I became CEO of a public internet company, just before the internet's boom as internet stock values increased dramatically (+800 percent). This was followed in 2000–2001 with what became known as "dot-bomb" as dot-com stocks' declined (-800 percent), making 1998–2001 the dot-com bubble. For me, dot-bomb wasn't just something I read about. This 800 percent decline became the most devastating business trial of my life. It is God's faithful work of blessing in my heart, through brokenness, that I want to share.

I had experienced an uninterrupted series of business successes, advancing to top executive leadership of an established public technology services company. I was a mature Christian and an elder in my church. I had sought to apply biblical principles to business as I used the gifts God had given me to provide for my family and be personally fulfilled in my business career. I agreed to become CEO of a small internet company that had gone public but was really struggling. This decision was based on a longstanding desire to more directly apply the gifts God had given me to building the kingdom of God. The opportunity to be CEO of this company fit because it was a Christian internet company. At that time, it was called Didax, Inc., which we later rebranded to Crosswalk.com (NASDAQ: AMEN). It was founded by fine Christian people who focused on ministry to Christians on the internet through the creation of an online Christian community.

Dot-Boom

When I arrived, the clock was ticking. While I knew my business gifts were from God and I was there because God had led me there, in my heart of hearts this was about me applying my gifts to create a successful Christian business. So off I went! We developed an aggressive strategy to leverage our strengths to market opportunity while creating corporate value, consistent with the basis for value that was being applied to internet companies at that time. We worked very hard over the next nine months in executing this strategy, and we began to see it succeed in incredible ways. We rebranded everything from Didax to Crosswalk.com and set out to provide all of life on the internet from a Christian perspective.

In ten short months, we had rocked the Christian world. Crosswalk.com had become the largest Christian presence on the internet and was rated in the top twenty-five internet sites in the world by Nielsen Net Ratings in the "Family and Lifestyle" category. Our market capitalization soared from literally zero to over $150 million. We were running network TV commercials in prime time, I had been on CNBC twice, had feature articles in *USA Today* and *Business Week*. At the time I thought this was a huge breakthrough for the kingdom of God and a great testimony to a world that was actually watching!

Dot-Broken

However, the hard work required to meet the expectations of my plan and the stress that mounted as I faced huge business issues, over which I really had little control, took its toll. I found myself almost paralyzed by sleep deprivation and an overwhelming responsibility to the people, the business, and the ministry. After agonizing for weeks, I went to my board of directors with a plan to drastically cut the staff in an attempt to dive toward a sustainable business not dependent on the craziness of the internet economy. This represented a total abandonment of my strategy and the beginning of the end of my vision for Crosswalk.com.

During that time, I found myself alone weeping or shouting out in anguish over the reality of my miserable failure. And I began to have periodic chest pains that peaked in a hospital emergency room. It was there, not knowing if I was approaching the end of my life, that I reached the end of myself and was truly broken. This brokenness was not of my choosing; it had been done to me. I confessed my sins in all the "little things," my lack of faith, my deception, my pride, and my selfishness. I knew I had nothing of myself and that anything of any value whatsoever was given to me by my great God. I had gone from hotshot Christian business executive, leading a public company to soaring corporate value, with CNBC appearances, network television commercials, tremendous visibility in both the Christian world and secular world, to business failure in the course of fourteen months.

From that point there was a new and very real humility that I applied to leading the business. There was also relief from the crushing stress I had felt for months. Now this isn't to say the business went well from that point on. In fact, quite the contrary: business went from really bad to about ten times worse.

As you can see, these were not cheap lessons by any means. This was not a fictional book illustration or some MBA exercise. We were working with real money and real lives. Think about it: millions in capital, thousands of investors, over a hundred employees, dear friends wounded and hurt, real anguish, real tears, real sleeplessness, real chest pains, a real hospital bill, and a real business failure.

You don't have to go through all this to learn brokenness. The US economy can't absorb too many failures as big as mine. It's God's will that you be broken, yet without the expense and suffering.

Learning Brokenness from David

Like I said before, you will be wise to learn brokenness from the examples of others! The remaining pages of this chapter will be spent examining brokenness from the life of David in its two interrelated facets, both reinforced throughout the New Testament, and its effects on the business. Press in. Take notes. Apply something!

Humbled by Your Honest (Often) Need for God's Forgiveness

As we considered in the last chapter, when you follow David's example and are really honest about your sin, you must often go to God for forgiveness and cleansing. This attitude of going often to God for forgiveness enhances your sense of dependence, increases your humility, and contributes to an honest experience of brokenness. The heart after God's heart draws us to this reality: if we are going to live in the conscious presence of God (seeking that one thing!), we *will* often go to God for forgiveness. There is no way, through our own performance, for us to consciously experience this life in the holy place of His presence. David understood! In Psalm 51, he first confesses and seeks restoration and acknowledges that his *sacrifices*, his efforts, his religious acts, his diligence, his self-deprivation, and even his great deeds in the name of God would not bring him to the experience of God's presence to receive His power for His intentions in business. Only David's brokenness—his emptying himself of all dependence on anything in his own power and ability—could bring him to this experience of the presence of almighty God for His purposes. And only through your dependence on God's work of grace and mercy, practically applied in all humility as you submit to His cleansing examination of your heart, can you do business in the power of His conscious presence.

This brokenness is a by-product of forgiveness as this brokenness is built on our need to go very often for forgiveness. Think about it. A spirit within you that is quick to defend your thoughts and actions to your conscience is hardly a broken spirit. A spirit that is not laid open and bare before the scriptures or seeking the Holy Spirit's examination is hardly a broken spirit. But a spirit that is really honest about sin, and open to the Holy Spirit and the scriptures, is a broken spirit. If this remains your honest attitude for a prolonged period of time and you continue to simply go to God in complete dependence for cleansing, you will experience the brokenness expressed in Psalm 51 from a heart after God's heart.

Identification with Christ's Death

The second facet of brokenness we learn from David is one that comes from believing we have been crucified with Christ. By faith, we are to consider ourselves dead to self and sin. David provides an example for us in an amazing, prophetic way when he looked ahead and identified with the crucifixion of Christ. Even speaking Christ's words in His death on the cross. "Into Your hand I commit my spirit" (Psalm 31:5).

Jesus Christ, God in the flesh, was broken; He suffered and died a cruel death. And David, centuries before Christ's birth, identified with Christ's brokenness in an amazing and supernaturally prophetic way. In this way, as much as any other, David demonstrated that indeed he did have a heart after God's heart.

In identifying with Christ's brokenness, David reveals the facet of brokenness that differs from our discussion of the brokenness proceeding from his frailty and his total dependence on God for forgiveness and cleansing, as we saw with his example in Psalm 51. Identifying with Christ's brokenness here is found in the spiritual participation in Christ's experience of personal crucifixion and death. As David prophetically said, "I am poured out like water, and all my bones are out of joint; my heart is like wax; it is melted within me ... they pierced my hands and my feet" (Psalm 22:14–16). The heart of David didn't just say these words; his heart really was broken as he identified with the Messiah. Remember whom we are talking about here. This is not some weird monk seeking to hurt himself to prove his devotion. This is King David. The great warrior ... the great ruler ... the great leader with whom we identify. Our purpose is to examine his heart revealed in the psalms and to understand what made that heart a heart after God's heart. Understanding this, we then seek to apply it to our hearts, as business leaders. Here we've learned, however, something we can't really understand: the heart of King David experienced the crucifixion of Jesus Christ! How is it possible to share this experience with David?

"I have been crucified with Christ." The same Holy Spirit who prompted David's identification with Christ's crucifixion also prompted the apostle Paul to identify with the crucifixion of Christ. "I have been crucified with Christ; and it is no longer I who live, but Christ lives in me; and the life which I now live in the flesh I live by faith in the Son of God, who loved me and gave Himself up for me" (Galatians 2:20).

Just as David went on to do God's business after his words of identification with the crucifixion of Christ in Psalm 22, so Paul went on to "live by faith in the Son of God" after identifying with Christ's crucifixion. From this we understand that identifying with Christ's crucifixion was not just because of David's unique position in the line of Christ or as a "type" of Christ. David did it. Paul did it. But how do you and I do it?

We identify with Christ's crucifixion by faith. We believe that when we received Christ as our Savior, we received His payment for our sins on the cross and *we also* identified with His death on the cross. While we don't physically die, by spiritually identifying with Christ's death, we have faith that we are dead to sin and to self. And considering ourselves dead to sin, we by faith mentally and emotionally close the door to self and sin and live only for Christ. Identifying with Christ brings us to this brokenness. Christians *talk* about living a life of faith. Our crucifixion with Christ is one of the things that we are to have faith in daily.

David did this by looking ahead in an amazing way to Christ's crucifixion and applying his identification with Christ's death to a current experience of his daily life. Paul did this by looking back to Christ's crucifixion and applying his identification with Christ's death to his current experience. And in Romans 6, the Holy Spirit through Paul gives the clear exhortation for you and me to look back and identify with Christ's death and apply it, by faith to our own lives.

> Our old self was crucified with Him, in order that our body of sin might be done away with, so that we would no longer be slaves to sin; for he who has died is freed from sin … For the death that He died, He died to sin once for all; but the life that He lives, He lives to God. Even so consider yourselves to be dead to sin, but alive to God in Christ Jesus. Therefore do not let sin reign in your mortal body so that you obey its lusts, and do not go on presenting the members of your body to sin as instruments of unrighteousness. (Romans 6:5–13)

Our crucifixion with Christ is not some great work of ours, or some great personal spiritual accomplishment, but it is the simple belief that we really have been crucified with Christ. It has already occurred. It is our belief in *all* that Christ did on the cross for us. It's faith in the reality of what transpired when we were saved. Now there is real brokenness in believing we really did die with Christ and as a result are dead to sin and self, but it's not some huge act of the will. It's simply an act of faith in what Christ has *already* done. This kind of brokenness is not some bag full of bad deals, but it is God's very best for us. In this brokenness we find true happiness that the world cannot affect. In fact, Jesus tells us, "Blessed [happy!] are the poor in spirit, for theirs is the kingdom of heaven" (Matthew 5:3).

As we consider faith in our identification with Christ's brokenness and His death, be encouraged to know that Christ's brokenness experience ended with His glorification. "Being found in appearance as a man, He humbled Himself by becoming obedient to the point of death, even death on a cross. For this reason also, God highly exalted Him, and bestowed on Him the name which is above every name" (Philippians 2:9). Christ was called the Son of David, and David's brokenness experience ended in the birth of Solomon and the line of Christ's blessing to all humankind for all eternity. You and I don't know the specific blessings that God has for us as we have faith in our death with Christ. As we yield to Him, however, we can expect His guidance to blessing in our business and personal life in ways we could never imagine or plan for ourselves.

The Impact of a Broken Business Leader

The effect of these two facets of brokenness is to make us open and tender toward God's work in our hearts and much less susceptible to sin. King David expressed this tender closeness to God this way. "The LORD is near to the brokenhearted and saves those who are crushed in spirit" (Psalm 34:18).

In business, we are conditioned to expect leaders should come in the same way the Jews expected their Messiah to come. They expected a great King and a conquering Messiah! What the Jews received though was God in the flesh—born as a baby and dying as a crucified Lord.

In Philippians 2 we are exhorted to brokenness by Christ's example.

> Have this attitude in yourselves which was in Christ Jesus,
> who ... emptied Himself ... humbled Himself ... to the
> point of death, even death on a cross. For this reason also,
> God highly exalted Him, and bestowed on Him the name
> which is above every name. (Philippians 2:5–9)

God highly exalted Christ because of Christ's brokenness leading to His humble sacrifice for humankind. Not only this, but we also know that

Christ's willingness to be broken for us directly resulted in immeasurable blessing of all humankind. Following Jesus's example of brokenness puts us on the pathway leading to the power, blessing, guidance, and indeed the exaltation of the God of the universe. These blessings from God certainly include business, but they transcend business, affecting every area of our lives.

Positioned to Lead

A business leader who maintains an attitude of brokenness by humbly going often to God for forgiveness—and then has faith that he is dead to sin and self—is positioned to lead business with a clear conscience, happily dependent on the God of the universe. Anyone in the world would recognize this business leader is centered and ready to confidently address the uncertainties of the business day. This is a changed business leader, and this kind of leader will generate a change in the business.

    This business leader will lead with greater consistency, as the selfishness that breeds inconsistency will be taken out of the equation. Brokenness produces the personal depth and a strong inner compass that is required to produce consistent direction. From this foundation, the leader has the strength to lead consistently through the inevitable business trials. This strength will come from God as He is relied upon rather than self. This consistency leads to greater productivity and confidence on the part of the staff each day, and especially in times of difficulty.

    Decisions will be made based on seeking the best for the business and for others in the business rather than on what the leader's current view of best for self might be in each situation. Many variables go into business decisions and many are unique to the particular situation, industry, discipline, etc. For each decision, the business leader must first have pure motivation in order to effectively receive God's guidance in applying the gifts He has given. A broken business leader has taken selfish motivation out of play in the decision process and is therefore in position to make wise decisions. All this will be noticed and will contribute to a healthy business culture.

Impact on Employees

The staff will increasingly have confidence in the leader's approach and will progressively be more inclined to follow the leader's example. This example of selflessness is at the core of building a strong team in business. These days much has been written on the importance of teamwork in business and some have suggested approaches to developing this team-first orientation in the enterprise. Yet if the business leader does not model selflessly seeking to make others more effective, even at the expense of self, then who would expect it to appear in the staff? The reality is that we don't expect the staff to perform selflessly so we invent ways to manipulate the staff into behavior that puts the team above themselves. This deception can produce some great team performance, but it only lasts so long. We will discuss this further in chapter 9, "Real Team Building."

As we've already mentioned, business schools don't train leaders in honest selflessness, which they can then model to the staff. The source of true selflessness comes from true brokenness. This brokenness must start at the top. As it is consistently modeled and valued by leadership, it will be progressively more evident in the staff. As this happens, the business leader will lead toward greater productivity and efficiency. The business leader will model a heart after God's heart and begin to produce *Business after God's Heart.*

Broken and Blessed

In business we have tended to elevate pride and self-reliance as virtues that propel us toward success. Let me tell you I felt some real highs as CEO of a high-flying internet company. Learning real brokenness, however, was the great and sustaining blessing of the internet company experience and probably of my life. This brokenness has profoundly informed my business leadership as I now recognize God's economy is contrary to regular business expectations. The greatest Man to ever live was a broken, humble servant who sacrificed Himself for many others. Through this enormous work, we were all blessed, and He was exalted. And David was a leader with a heart after God's heart. He had a humble, broken heart, totally dependent on the Lord in his business, as he says in Psalm 22 and Psalm 28. "But I am a worm and not a man, a reproach of men and despised by the people …

Blessed be the Lord, because He has heard the voice of my supplication. The Lord is my strength and my shield; my heart trusts in Him, and I am helped; therefore my heart exults, and with my song I shall thank Him." This is the heart that God blessed. And as God blessed this heart, He also blessed those David led.

CHAPTER 4

God in Your Business Thoughts

O Lord, You have searched me and known
me …You understand my thought from afar.
—Psalm 139:1

Real Corporate Values Are Found in Corporate Thought Life

Smart companies spend a lot of time developing corporate values in order to influence the way employees think about the overall business and how they behave right from the core. This is done so consistently that in the over thirty years I've worked strategy with top-level executives, I have not once made it from the reception area to the main conference room without seeing the company's values displayed in some shape or form. Usually the values are contained on plaques or brochures, and normally they're expressed in some version of *"Integrity, Excellence, and Innovation."* While always done with the good intention of influencing how employees think about the company and their job, for employees this usually boils down to "Blah, blah, corporate-speak, blah, blah, blah."

In one such client-company with the obligatory "Values Plaque" on the wall, I pointed out to the president that the word "commitment" had been misspelled twice. He turned around to look at the plaque and then said, "You know, it's funny, that's been on all our conference room walls for over five years and no one has ever noticed that before. I guess nobody actually reads those things." And incredibly, the plaque remained unchanged in every conference room for the remainder of my consultancy!

Not all companies are this apathetic about communicating their corporate values. Great companies understand that what employees really think is of extreme importance because it determines what is said and done when no supervisors are around to watch. In the same way, what you really think is of extreme importance, because your business management and leadership flow from the core of your thoughts. You might say the heart of a business leader is found in his thoughts.

Our hero, King David, takes this matter of our business thought life to a whole different level. And through the psalms, David shows us that God has a plan to give us a level of power in our thinking that will completely transform our business leadership. He expresses this most succinctly in Psalm 139.

> O Lord, You have searched me and known me. You know when I sit down and when I rise up; You understand my thought from afar. You scrutinize my path and my lying down, And are intimately acquainted with all my ways. Even before there is a word on my tongue, Behold, O Lord, You know it all. You have enclosed me behind and before, And laid Your hand upon me. Such knowledge is too wonderful for me; It is too high, I cannot attain to it. (Psalm 139:1–6)

Our first lesson from the heart of David was that he sought one thing, as he said in Psalm 27. "One thing I have asked from the Lord, that shall I seek: That I may dwell in the house of the Lord all the days of my life, to behold the beauty of the Lord and to meditate in His temple … When You said, 'Seek My face,' my heart said to You, 'Your face, O Lord, I shall seek'" (Psalm 27:4, 8). We were inspired with David to follow his example in seeking the Lord; to consciously enjoy the riches of fellowship with the God of the universe that Christ came to provide. Now in Psalm 139, David takes us to a deeper understanding of God's initiative, apart from our desire to seek Him, as He is constantly, persistently, engaging in our thought lives. So as we seek that one thing, to consciously dwell in His presence, He is right there already in the midst of our thoughts. Through this added, overlapping dimension of inspired awareness, the heart of David leads our hearts to a depth of devotion, stability, and confidence to further empower and bless our leadership.

God in the Midst of Your Business Thinking

In fact, we see in Psalm 139 that God not only understood "his thought from afar" but also had knowledge of David's thoughts that would become words, as he says, "even before there is a word on my tongue, behold, O Lord, You know it all." David also said that in addition to God being in the midst of his thoughts and words, He was also fully engaged as those thoughts led to actions. "You scrutinize my path and my lying down, and are intimately acquainted with all my ways."

The same is true for us in business. Embracing God's presence in our thoughts as David did means we also embrace His presence as we begin to develop our business words and business actions. And His presence, as it is there in our thoughts that form our words and our actions, is full of His grace, mercy, power, and knowledge! Our conscious faith in God's engagement here should produce great confidence and consistency between our thoughts, words, and actions that is clearly God's design.

In this regard, David invites God's examination of his thoughts in Psalm 26:2. "Examine me, O Lord, and try me; test my mind and my heart." Notice David connects his mind with his heart, and he asks God to engage right there.

Recognizing Our Deceitfulness

Deceit is a symptom of lack of fidelity between your thoughts and your words or actions. David goes on in Psalm 26 to speak about deceit in verses 4 and 5. "I do not sit with deceitful men, nor will I go with pretenders. I hate the assembly of evildoers, and I will not sit with the wicked." If your words and actions are not consistent with your thoughts, then you are a "pretender." In Psalm 26 David connects the pretenders and deceitful to evildoers.

In business, most leaders (including Christians) would not want to expose their real thoughts in their words. So leaders in business often speak to manipulate behavior and create perceptions (or more accurately, deceptions). If we feel forced to do this, it's because we have not acknowledged and embraced God's presence in our thoughts.

We have our thoughts that are really driving our business, and God is not recognized in the midst of those thoughts. Then we have the thoughts of God that we have at church, in our devotionals, or even in times of prayer during the business day. Because we have not acknowledged God's presence in *every* thought, however, we have effectively become a pretender or "double-hearted" person.

Before you dismiss the application of Psalm 26 to your own heart, let's think for a moment. Do your words of encouragement to your subordinates, peers, or superiors come from an honest heart of unconditional love for them, or do they come from a heart that seeks to manipulate behavior? Are your relationships with potential clients driven by God's love and Christian service, or are you pretending to care in order to make a sale?

David goes deeper into thought life as he speaks of the issue of a "double heart" in Psalm 12:1–3.

> Help, LORD, for the godly man ceases to be, for the faithful disappear from among the sons of men. They speak falsehood to one another; with flattering lips and with a double heart they speak. May the LORD cut off all flattering lips, the tongue that speaks great things.

If you can effectively fake Christian love, you will make a lot of friends and influence a lot of people. But are you "speaking falsehood to one another; with flattering lips and with a double heart?" David points out that the godly person, who does not have a double heart, "disappears" (verse 1). In other words, the real straight shooter has always been a rarity. The godly straight shooter's thought life (heart) is a pure heart—thoughts laid bare and aware of the active engagement of God with all His love, grace, mercy, and power—and the words this person says reflect God's active engagement inside his or her thought life. The godly straight shooter only has one heart and it has been made pure. From this heart come his or her words. When we feel a need to make our words different from our thoughts (our hearts), we are actually alerted to a need to address our hearts. Then rather than speak and act from a double heart, we get our heart right as we seek God's grace, mercy, and restoration. In other words, we return to our pure heart, and it is made that way by applying the blood of Christ.

David's awareness of God's presence, love, and power in his every business thought is indeed a rare experience for most Christian business leaders. We come from a Christian culture tending to separate our walk with God from our walk in the office corridors. We may think this separation is a function of Equal Employment Opportunity (EEO) laws of our time. Or we might subconsciously buy into this legal separation our culture has drilled into our minds to the extent of reinforcing this separation even in our thought life. It is easy to sincerely seek God's blessing in business on one level yet still feel this divide between our devotional life and our business life. We attend church, we may be a leader in the church, we even tithe, and things seem to be going great. Since we don't recognize His presence in our every business thought to help and guide us, just as He engaged in David's thoughts, we pray for blessing and then set out on our own. To this prayer we may add legalistic Christian formulae for business success. In the end though, we perform our moment-by-moment business functions far from the conscious realization of God's presence in all our business thoughts. All this doesn't help us to get to the bottom of heart or thought-life issues, and we consequently don't experience the real power and love of God practically in our business leadership as David did.

David's Psalms Reveal God's Better Plan

God's best for us is to embrace the reality of His presence in every business thought. It's for us to have fidelity as our thoughts turn into words and actions. And His best for us is for His power and love, present in all our thoughts, to shape our day-to-day business leadership very practically.

Real Awareness of God in Every Thought

The Spirit uses David through his psalms to give us a level of power in our thinking that will completely transform our business leadership. We tend to think if God connects with a business, He connects from the outside like some kind of lightning strike. In reality, the wonderful and amazing truth is that He actually connects with a business through His engagement within the thought life of business leaders. As we actively recognize God's engagement here—in our thoughts, where words and actions begin—we will be excited each moment as we experience God working through our hearts to touch our businesses very practically. From David's inspired leadership, we can see how powerfully this can work.

David's Awareness of God in His Thoughts

Sometimes we rationalize that God is only in the thoughts to which we invite Him or He is only there when we are aware of His presence as we think. In Psalm 139, David understands and expresses the truth that God is in the midst of every thought—even before the thought is expressed as language. "You understand my thought from afar. You scrutinize my path and my lying down, And are intimately acquainted with all my ways. Even before there is a word on my tongue, Behold, O LORD, You know it all." David was inspired to see that God was in all his thoughts as he led Israel to great conquests and as he managed God's people. What a great comfort David had as he considered the magnitude of his responsibilities! What encouragement as he realized the impact that God's participation in all his thoughts would have on God's people and God's purposes as those thoughts led to actions in leading God's enterprise.

Is This a Thought Invasion?

If your reaction to the truth that God almighty is in the midst of your every thought is fear, denial, and/or futile resistance, then you miss the blessing God intends for you. The image you have of God's presence in your every thought may resemble God as some sort of security guard who invades your mental privacy by monitoring a bank of TV screen images, taking notes on all your thought activity, and keeping records for a future accounting. This is not what the Spirit tells us through David in Psalm 139.

Instead, the image should be of your intimate Father who loves you unconditionally and beyond any ability to measure. David clearly expressed in Psalm 139 this concept of God's love and care in the midst of each thought. While expressing his awareness of God's knowledge of the details of every thought, David also says in verse 4, "You have enclosed me behind and before, and laid Your hand upon me." While God is engaged in every thought, His infinite love and sovereign power have everything covered around you. With His participation in each of your thoughts, God almighty has "enclosed [you] behind and before" with His protection, and He has "laid His hand upon [you]" with all His love and care.

Inside each of your thoughts you are loved, protected, and cared for, consistent with Christ's work at Calvary. The Spirit tells us in Romans 5:8, "But God demonstrates His own love toward us in that while we were yet sinners, Christ died for us." Christ's infinite and unconditional love was demonstrated at Calvary, but it didn't stop at Calvary. The personal love for you so evident when Jesus hung on the cross was a demonstration of God's exact same love He has for you in the midst of your each and every thought. As a thought flashes through your mind in this very moment, God is loving you with the same intensity of *unconditional* love that He had for you personally at Calvary.

You don't have to get the thought right or make it proper in order for God to love you that way. His love is just there with that thought, as surely as His presence is there. While you were still a sinner, Christ died for you to demonstrate the kind of love He would have for you eternally. And now, while you yet have a sinful thought, Christ is just as much there in that thought with His infinite and unconditional love, so perfectly demonstrated and proven at Calvary. He demonstrated it. He proved it. So you would have faith His love really is there now, in the thought that you are having right now, and in the next moment. Enjoy His proven, unconditional, infinite love in the thought you're having right now. It's there for you. He's there with that love right now and so on for the rest of your life! Amazingly, from Psalm 139, we know that David understood the engagement of God almighty in his thought life, with all His love and care, and it transformed his leadership from the core of his being.

This Awareness Changes Everything

This awesome and overpowering truth is almost incomprehensibly great! In fact, as David meditates on God's presence in his thoughts with His unconditional love and care, he says, "Such knowledge is too wonderful for me; It is too high, I cannot attain to it." Faith in the way He loves you within each of your thoughts should make you feel the same way; it's just "too wonderful" for each one of us! Such knowledge is so wonderful that it transforms your countenance. Such knowledge of God's unconditional love in the midst of each and every thought compels us to God. It compels us to welcome and embrace His presence in our business thoughts. And this awareness of God's presence in our thought life changes our mental setup as we begin thinking about the issues of our business.

David Needed a Clean Conscience to Be Effective

From David's inspired perspective of God's presence in his thoughts from Psalm 139, we're drawn back to Psalm 51 where David sees his heart as the combination of all his thoughts and emotions and asks God to "create in [him] a clean heart." We know this is an inspired prayer and by recognizing God's presence in our thoughts we can practically see how it can work for you and me. We've discussed Psalm 51 as a psalm of confession, repentance, and restoration, but here we see how David focuses on the depths of his thought life as he reveals one of the keys to a heart after God's heart. "Behold, You desire truth in the innermost being, and in the hidden part You will make me know wisdom. Purify me with hyssop, and I shall be clean; wash me, and I shall be whiter than snow" (Psalm 51:6–7). In acknowledging God's desire for "truth in my innermost being," David is acknowledging God's desire for truth, or fidelity, at the core of his thought life. As we've already seen in Psalm 139, David knew well the engagement of God in his thoughts, even his "innermost being." In Psalm 51, however, David associates God's engagement in his thought life and His desire for "truth" at the core of David's thoughts with David's need for God's cleansing.

There is no way for David, or me, you, or anyone else, to have real truth at the core of our thought life except through applying Christ's blood to cleanse each sinful thought. The great news is through the blood of Jesus, you can be made pure and be given truth at the core of where your thoughts begin. You *can* have a clean heart.

Your Business Thinking Needs Christ's Purifying Blood

This is to be a practical experience in business. David encourages us to remain conscious of God's presence inside every thought and maintain the purity of our thoughts through the practical application of God's grace so there can be real fidelity between our thoughts, our words, and our actions. As he put it in Psalm 15:1–2, "O Lord, who may abide in Your tent? Who may dwell on Your holy hill? He who walks with integrity, and works righteousness, and *speaks truth in his heart*" (emphasis mine). This fidelity between thought, word, and action can indeed be practically experienced by the business leader, but only by honestly applying the blood of Christ to our thought life. No rationalization of the thought. No justification of the thought. No denial of the thought. There's just a broken acknowledgment and confession of the deceitful, dishonest, proud, greedy, selfish, faithless, unloving, impatient, bitter, or hateful thought. Our acknowledgment is not news to God because He has already been present in your thoughts all the time! He has been there ready to forgive and completely restore our thinking consistent with His unconditional love and immediately restore from the moment anything other than "truth in my innermost being" happened.

This is not a matter of quickly correcting your thoughts and by force of your will making yourself think better thoughts. It's a matter of simply receiving God's free gift of forgiveness and His *complete* cleansing as applied to the bad thought. It's not recovering your thinking; it's getting grace for your thinking. It's getting grace right there at the point of God's continual engagement in your thoughts. Trying to recover your thinking is a futile work of the flesh. You will never get all the way there, and you'll just be discouraged and want to try to flee from the reality of God's presence in your thoughts. So don't try to recover your thinking; get His grace and mercy for your thinking. His grace and mercy are divinely powerful and effective to restore at the core of where you begin to think "in your innermost being" (Psalm 51:6).

As we've discussed before, you will be perpetually dependent on Him and His grace as you go to Him often, instead of relying on your ability to improve your thinking in some futile attempt to make yourself holy. Holiness can only come by Christ's work, not by your own. And holiness will come, because practicing His presence in your thoughts and going often for grace and forgiveness progressively improve your thinking. Having just confessed thoughts, you are not as likely to go back there quickly. Bad thought habits are rooted out through honest confession and repentance, and when your thinking improves by His grace, you begin to more practically experience the holiness given by God's grace. In all of this, He "creates in [you] a clean heart." And with David, humility with power (God's power) take shape at your core.

"Truth in my innermost being"—a totally clean conscience—is a powerful asset for a business leader. And a totally clean conscience is exactly what God offers through the blood of Christ, as His blood is applied to our thought life. In Psalm 51 we see that David found this. He found it, not as a result of his perfect performance. In fact, quite the contrary. David found the power of a clean conscience out of his brokenness over sin and complete dependence on God for cleansing. In gaining a clean conscience, the business leader, with David, is also able to lead with confidence at the core of his being. This confidence is not manufactured through some mind game, nor is it a by-product of arrogant pride. Instead, it is a confidence born of faith in the effectiveness of the blood of Jesus Christ applied to our thoughts.

Emotionally Stable Leadership

When you accept and acknowledge God's presence in your business thoughts, it produces emotional stability and contributes to a stable business. We've all been around leaders who wear their emotions on their sleeve, such as a quick temper leading to outbursts of anger. Most of our emotions run deeper than this, however, and are not necessarily seen in such an obvious outward manifestation. Emotions, whether obvious or not, do play a role in the way you manage and the decisions you make. When we have hidden feelings of hatred toward a subordinate, it affects the way we engage with that subordinate. When we are grieved by a business setback, it affects our countenance and tone of voice with a peer. When we've been hurt by a personal attack, we may feel an irrational desire to settle the score and make a bad decision.

Let's think for a moment about the source of our emotions. Our emotions proceed from the point where our thoughts begin. Our feelings are shaped by a set of thoughts converging at a point in time in our minds. If we are having real faith in God's engagement in every thought with His infinite and unconditional love, it will clearly affect our emotional setup. It will affect the way we feel about the things that are going on around us in business. Faith in God's unconditional love for you in the midst of each and every thought you have, no matter what that thought is, puts a smile on your face; it affects you emotionally. God almighty loves you personally beyond all measure and His love for you is totally proven by Christ's work. And that love is very active in this present thought! When your emotional stability is anchored in this truth, you are emotionally stable indeed.

God has given our emotions to us for His purposes. Having said that, we can be certain His purpose in giving us these emotions was not so that we would sin. Instead, it is so He can use our emotions to prompt, guide, and propel us to His purposes, including His purposes in business. If our thoughts are our own, however, and they include unconfessed sinful thoughts, then all these bad thoughts combine to create emotions not generated by God but are of the flesh, sinful, and evil. A business led by a person unwittingly driven by sinful emotions is a business being prompted and guided to the wrong places. On the other hand, as we are conscious of His engagement in our thoughts, and submitted to His love, power, and cleansing right in the midst of each thought, then our emotions are formed by His righteous hand and for His purposes. From here we are in position to give emotional strength and stability to our employees and our business. We are "centered" business leaders, able to assimilate good and bad news in a way that inspires confidence in the midst of the uncertainties of business and our passions are stirred to lead to God's blessings.

Even in the Midst of Despair

Things go wrong in business. Some things go radically wrong. Some bad things that happen are totally beyond our control and some bad things we actually help cause. The reality is "stuff" happens. You can count on it. And business leaders can feel the emotional weight of hopelessness and despair like anyone else.

When a business leader feels despair, although it can be concealed by leaders who are good at deception, it affects the leader's entire enterprise. It can be denied and held in but will still have a substantial effect on the leader and the organization. For the leader, prolonged despair can yield depression and all its accompaniments. Hidden despair on the part of the business leader may not look like despair to the organization, but the staff will likely feel the effect of overreaction and/or total inaction as decisions are driven by inordinate fear or a sense of helplessness. For the organization, the business leader's despair yields uneasiness, fear, and even panic, with all the associated negative impact on productivity.

Even the best and most godly business leaders at times feel despair in business. Sometimes it's a fleeting feeling, and other times it persists. Our hero, King David, certainly was subject to despair, as is exposed through many of his psalms.

David's Despair and Recognition of God

If you read Psalm 42, you'll notice first that David has an honest sense for his thoughts and his emotions. The condition of his heart is summed up in verse 11. "Why are you in despair, O my soul? And why have you become disturbed within me? Hope in God, for I shall yet praise Him, The help of my countenance and my God." He knows what he is really thinking, and he knows despair when he feels it in his heart. Notice that David does not deny his despair and he doesn't try to cover it up. He recognizes his emotions for what they are, so he can receive God's treatment for his heart.

After David's sense for his thoughts makes apparent his heart is feeling despair, he applies his knowledge of God to his heart or his thoughts. David applied the truth to his emotion and chose to have faith in that truth, as he says these words to himself: "Hope in God, for I shall again praise Him for the help of His presence." David feels despair. He adds faith in God's presence to his thoughts, knowing this faith will help him be restored emotionally into a position of real praise from an honest heart.

The combination of thoughts that lead to a feeling of despair cannot build up a head of steam in the midst of real faith in God's personal love and power applied to those very thoughts. David's faith in the truth about God's character present in his thoughts brought peace at the core of his being—where he begins to think—and put David in position to continue being effective in leadership. And so it shall be for you and me.

Greater Depth for Even Greater Stability

The heart of David takes us deeper still in Psalm 139, anchoring our thoughts and our emotions in God's glorious engagement at the very core of our thought formation for business leadership. David goes on to say in Psalm 139:13–17,

For You formed my inward parts; You wove me in my
mother's womb. I will give thanks to You, for I am
fearfully and wonderfully made; wonderful are Your
works, and my soul knows it very well. My frame was
not hidden from You, when I was made in secret, and
skillfully wrought in the depths of the earth; Your eyes
have seen my unformed substance; and in Your book
were all written the days that were ordained for me,
when as yet there was not one of them.

Your loving God who is present in your thoughts formed you. He's
not just getting to know you, even though you may feel you're just
getting to know Him. He's been intimately and *powerfully* engaged
at your very core to *make you*. ("Your eyes have seen my unformed
substance ... You formed my inward parts.") He created you to be
His temple and He did not walk away but instead lives actively and
powerfully within you. He made you to be His eternal son or daughter
and He *stays engaged not only for eternity but for this business day!* As
sure as He started with your "unformed substance," He has been, and
is, sovereignly engaged with love and power within you, His temple.
David calls us to faith right there. God's engagement in our thoughts
flows from His creative power that formed us to be His forever. Real
faith, certainty, of God's personal and individual exercise of His
power, commitment, and eternal purpose yields a certain expectation
of continued practical engagement that is manifest in our thought life.
God's engagement in our thought life is as sure as His engagement to
create in us the ability to think. He created in us that ability to think
and He stayed engaged as He will always be there with us. ("Where
can I go from Your Spirit? Or where can I flee from Your presence?
If I ascend to heaven, You are there." Psalm 139:7–8.) This very
deep foundation for our day-to-day thinking generates tremendous
emotional stability for leadership. This was foundational for David
and as he shares his heart, we hear the Spirit exhort us to *embrace faith
in our hearts* for this depth of God's continued practical engagement
in our thinking each day.

Your Business Judgments from God's Presence

Recognizing God's presence in your business thoughts brings God's power to your business thoughts. When you have an image of God being outside yourself, you think you can talk to God on your terms. You think you can turn Him on and turn Him off like a TV show or your cell phone. You think you can seek Him when you need Him and separately enjoy whatever mental playground you've established related to your business leadership. This image of God in your life deprives you of the *power* of God in your thoughts as you lead.

Your thoughts are where you really live. And your thoughts are certainly the base from which you lead your business. If you can experience God's participation in your business thoughts as we have discussed, then you have accessed the almighty God of the universe at the point where business leadership begins! From this foundation comes the power of God in King David. This is the power for godly leadership. And this is the foundation for greatness, God's greatness, working through the business leader just as He did through King David.

As we've seen in Psalm 139, David says God engages His power and knowledge to "enclose [him] behind and before" with His comprehensive strength. As we embrace the presence of God's *power* in all our thoughts, along with His love and care, we are strengthened at the core of our soul. This is something to be excited about. This is something that should give us great confidence as we enter each business day and each business encounter. What an amazing gift!

David prayed, "Let my judgment come forth from Your presence" (Psalm 17:2). God wants to answer this inspired prayer of David's for you also. As you embrace God's engagement directly in your thoughts with His power, strength, and guidance, you can have real confidence that your business judgments are coming from His presence. This is the substantive engagement of almighty God in your heart, your innermost thoughts, for real greatness. This most powerful asset is central for the business leader to develop *Business after God's Heart*.

CHAPTER 5

Gaining God's Business Guidance

I will instruct you and teach you in
the way which you should go; I will
counsel you with My eye upon you.
—Psalm 32:8

Motivation for Guidance

We all want God's guidance in our business. I have never talked to a Christian businessperson who didn't express a desire for God's guidance and blessing in business. If most of us are honest though, our core motivation for asking God's guidance is ultimately selfish. It's about me. Ask yourself, "Do I really want to direct my business consistent with God's will? Or in my heart of hearts, am I actually directing my business consistent with my own desires and simply expecting God to follow along with His blessing?" I think this is a tough question for all of us.

David makes it clear that the practical matter of seeking and receiving God's guidance begins with our motivation for God's guidance. "For You are my rock and my fortress; for Your name's sake You will lead me and guide me" (Psalm 31:3). Notice that David's motivation for God's guidance is "for Your name's sake." Seeking the real, practical guidance of God almighty is a very serious endeavor, and we must first honestly ask ourselves about our motivation. This is a soul-searching exercise. Can you honestly say that you are seeking God's guidance in business for His "name's sake," that is, for His honor or His glory?

God as a "Lucky Charm"

When it's really about me and mine, in one way or another I treat God like some kind of "lucky charm." I basically do my own thing in business, relying on my own instincts and gifts, and just carry God along in hopes of improving my chances. Personally, I've seen this work out in the workplace in ways so extreme they were almost comical.

While CEO of Crosswalk.com, Inc., I met a Christian investment banker who was involved in taking a chain of strip joints public. Go figure! He also had a substantial interest in Crosswalk.com's publicly traded stock. I met him during the ebb and flow of the internet boom and bust, in the early days when Crosswalk.com's stock was down, before the stock's meteoric rise. He told me that although Crosswalk was down, every portfolio in which he had put Crosswalk.com stock was up significantly. He felt that God was blessing his other stock in the portfolio because of the Christian purpose and focus of Crosswalk.com. For all I know, he probably thought the strip joints did well just when in a portfolio including Crosswalk.com!

You won't ever find yourself in the same boat as this investment banker. However, I do think we often engage in a thought process similar to his. I know I have. Although we wouldn't say it out loud, we may subtly consider our relationship with God a way to get an edge in this very competitive business world. Maybe we don't actually want God's guidance in the day-to-day details of our business. We just want Him to help us do a little better than our competitors.

In fairness, many Christian business leaders do genuinely desire God's guidance for His glory but just don't understand how to make it practical. Issues and decisions confront us daily. Since God isn't writing any guidance in our credenza dust, we feel forced to strike out on our own wits, asking God to bless our efforts.

The encouraging reality is God has much more than this for us. Let's turn again to the heart of King David for very practical help in seeking and obtaining God's guidance in business.

"For Your Name's Sake You Will Lead Me and Guide Me"

Getting to the bottom of our motivation for seeking God's guidance is cleansing and clarifying. It gets us to where the action in our heart really is, gives us fidelity as we seek Him, and provides confidence as we move out. So let's ask ourselves, "Is this God's business or my business?" If it's really your own business or career and you are seeking God's guidance for yourself, then you have transitioned into subtly treating God like a "lucky charm" to bless your efforts, favor your desired outcome, or give you some kind of edge. In this regard, you must call sin by its name.

The very core of sin is self-centeredness. As you acknowledge this sin of selfishness, you can be immediately forgiven and cleansed completely. From this position of being made pure and holy by God's grace, through Christ's incredible work of love for you personally, you can respond with gratitude, love, and a sincere desire to receive God's guidance for His business that exists for His glory.

This takes us back to the whole issue of brokenness that we discussed in chapter 3. Brokenness involves your identification with the crucifixion of Christ. As we've discussed, in the midst of David's "business," he prophetically experienced this crucifixion. "I am poured out like water, and all my bones are out of joint; my heart is like wax; it is melted within me … they pierced my hands and my feet" (Psalm 22:14–16). And Paul also sets the example for us as he says in Galatians 2:20, "I have been crucified with Christ; and it is no longer I who live, but Christ lives in me; and the life which I now live in the flesh I live by faith in the Son of God, who loved me and gave Himself up for me."

If, by faith, you have been crucified with Christ, in one sense you don't have a business or a career. In fact, you are no longer living at all, but it's Christ that lives in you by faith. You have said with David, and with Christ, "Into Your hand I commit my Spirit" (Psalm 31:5). And from there on out, the life you have left is completely His. So while Christ really does live in you, and by faith you are dwelling in His presence, God has given you this job of leading His business. This is an extremely cool and confident place to be!

If your business or your career is still centered on you, God offers grace to solve that problem for you right where you are now. It's really simple, but it is humbling. Right now, seek His forgiveness and cleansing, and come confidently to Him, recognizing that your self-centeredness has been put to death, as it was nailed to the cross with Christ. Don't listen to the excuses or denials that may be flooding your mind right now, because the prospect of what was formerly your business actually becoming the personal business of God almighty is a very powerful and liberating prospect. And it should give you great confidence as you come to Him for guidance in the leadership of His business. This is the starting point in seeking God's guidance in business.

One Thing (Again!)

Not only did David recognize he was doing God's business, but his soul, the very core of his being, was consumed in seeking God Himself. "O God, You are my God, I shall seek You earnestly, my soul thirsts for You, my flesh yearns for You" (Psalm 63:1). In fact, we began our study by laying the foundation revealed in Psalm 27. "One thing I have asked from the Lord, that I shall seek: That I may dwell in the house of the Lord all the days of my life, to behold the beauty of the Lord and to meditate in His temple" (Psalm 27:4). So as we consider David's example in the pursuit of God's guidance in business, we must remember this core motivation of a heart after God's heart and examine again the motivation of our own heart.

As I seek God's guidance for His business, is my soul thirsting after God? Do I desire that one thing as David did: to consciously experience the presence of God almighty? Or have I become distracted or deceived, falling into the pursuit of wealth, promotion, personal success, or the pride of life? When my heart's motivation really is to seek God, thirsting after God and living in His presence, I have peace and confidence as I come to Him for guidance. If I come for guidance with other motivations at the heart of things, I may feel the need for His guidance, but that guidance is sought with an attitude of fretfulness, insecurity, and anxiety about the future. In that state we come to God for instant gratification or to gain a stamp of approval on our fleshly desires rather than a sincere and patient pursuit of guidance that comes as part of actively and consciously dwelling with Him.

Practically Seeking God's Guidance in Business

Having now followed David's heart in sorting out our motivations for guidance and setting all that straight, let's look at David's experience of practically receiving God's guidance in his business as he expressed in the psalms. His experience can be grouped in the following three general categories:

1. guidance from God's special revelation of His will through His Word
2. guidance in response to David's specific initiative
3. guidance as a result of God's clear initiative in David's life, in ways He might not have even been aware of

1. Business Guidance from God's Special Revelation, His Word

This great leader of God's business knew the Word of God. Just read the psalms of David and you know the heart after God's heart had a deep love for the Word. His sacred poetry is clear evidence that he was immersed in the scripture and the Word was the delight of his life. It is evident David found, through this immersion in the riches of God's Word, God's guidance for the business God had given him to lead.

> The law of the Lord is perfect, restoring the soul; the testimony of the Lord is sure making wise the simple. The precepts of the Lord are right, rejoicing the heart; the commandment of the Lord is pure, enlightening the eyes. The fear of the Lord is clean, enduring forever; the judgments of the Lord are true; they are righteous altogether. They are more desirable than gold, yes, than much fine gold; sweeter also than honey and the drippings of the honeycomb. Moreover, by them Your servant is warned; in keeping them there is great reward. (Psalm 19:7–11)

From this passage alone we understand how extremely valuable the Word of God is to the business leader who is seeking guidance. The Word restores the soul, makes wise the simple, rejoices the heart, enlightens the eyes, endures forever, and in keeping it there is great reward. As a result, the business leader who, like David, seeks God's guidance from His Word is refreshed, wise, happy, stable, and rewarded! Wouldn't it be great to be this guy? And wouldn't it be great to be led by this guy!

Clearly, God uses His Word to guide the business leader to wise decisions and wise courses of action. David wanted God's plans for God's enterprise. Nothing provides better stability for business than a foundation on the unchangeable, proven Word of God. David expressed this confidence in God's Word in Psalm 33:11. "The counsel of the Lord stands forever, the plans of His heart from generation to generation." This eternal Word of God guides as specific passages in the Word are brought to bear in relation to specific decisions. In addition, it guides as the weight of scripture's overall counsel is applied by considering many different passages from a leader's life of study and application of God's Word. David had studied the scriptures extensively and says, "I delight to do Your will, O my God; Your Law is within my heart" (Psalm 40:8). David had memorized and lived the Word to such an extent that it was "within [his] heart." As a result, David was guided by the Word in his mind, as he connected his knowledge of the Word to his business situation. We see from Psalm 19 that the Word, in an amazing way, can "enlighten the eyes" to see what others don't see. And from uncertainty and indecision, the Word brings the light needed to move forward with confidence as it steadies our footing in uncertain situations. Because the Word was in David's heart, he was stable as he led in God's business. "The law of his God is in his heart; His steps do not slip" (Psalm 37:31).

The Bible is not a business manual. As a practical matter, however, David's understanding and application of God's Word in business decision-making immediately removed many alternatives from the table. It narrowed his focus in prayer and in seeking God's specific guidance consistent with His special revelation clearly contained in scripture. The Word is relevant for us—whether it be in relation to something God has clearly addressed in His Word or by establishing principles that find application in the details of our business. For example, we don't have to wring our hands too long when asking these questions: Should I pay on time? Should I honor my contract? Should I keep my promises? Should I care about my employees' work environment? Should I be honest in my sales presentation? Should I misrepresent my financials? Should I honor my boss? For in situations like these, we have clear guidance from God through His Word; it becomes a question of obedience.

Then as we meditate on scripture and make the prayerful examination of God's Word part of our daily interaction with Him, the Holy Spirit applies His Word to our hearts in ways that make clear His direction in the business. "For the Word of God is living and active and sharper than any two-edged sword, and piercing as far as the division of soul and spirit, of both joints and marrow, and able to judge the thoughts and intentions of the heart" (Hebrews 4:12). In our devotions or Bible study, we remain open to God's engagement in our hearts for the business we lead and all areas of our life. Since work consumes an extremely large percentage of our time that we're awake, we're either directly applying our study of the Word of God to our business or we are hardly applying it to our life at all. And as the living Word of God "pierces" into our lives, He applies it to our business thoughts and decisions in ways the Holy Spirit prompts and in ways that may not have been clear from previous readings of even the same passage. In this way, God provides guidance in business as we remain tender and obedient to these promptings from His Word.

God's Word is tried and true through the ages, and David founded his enterprise on the reliability of the Word, as he said in Psalm 12:6. "The words of the Lord are pure words; as silver tried in a furnace on the earth, refined seven times. You, O Lord, will keep them; You will preserve him from this generation forever." Simply applying the proven Word of God to business will make one wise in business. According to David in Psalm 19, it will also make one abidingly happy at the core of your being ("rejoicing the heart"). So as we apply God's Word to our business situations, we should expect God to "enlighten our eyes," give us insights, and bless our decisions for His glory. And from Psalm 19 we understand the exciting truth: by keeping His Word "there is great reward." Now if our focus and motivation is on God's glory, we will be sincerely open to this reward coming in ways that may not be financial or even temporal. As we apply His Word to business, however, we should have real faith He will bring real rewards to our life. So applying faith in His Word, we should do business in a manner that reflects a confident expectation of reward.

2. God's Business Guidance in Response to Our Prayers

There are plenty of situations in business that our knowledge of scripture does not directly address. For example, judgments on the effectiveness of people in the roles they are assigned is a regular challenge for the business leader. Making judgments and decisions in this arena have enormous impact on the enterprise as well as individuals. Because of these impacts, decisions in this area are often extremely difficult to make. Yet unless there is some kind of moral failure on the part of people involved, these decisions are seldom a cut-and-dried application of some scripture text. Even so, the business leader must confront these situations and make decisions on a regular basis.

Once again, let's look to God's hand in David's life. King David, having taken guidance from God consistent with his knowledge of God and His Word, gives us a great example of seeking God's guidance in areas of uncertainty. In Psalm 25:4–5, we see David come confidently to God, praying for guidance. "Make me know Your ways, O Lord; teach me Your paths. Lead me in Your truth and teach me, for You are the God of my salvation; for You I wait all the day." Clearly, David has God's Word yet he is praying for guidance and "waiting all the day" for God to lead him.

Here we see the heart after God's heart actively seeking guidance from God almighty in areas where judgments are not clear from the scripture. Praying for God's guidance would seem to be an obvious step in gaining God's guidance in business. In the fast-paced, self-sufficient world of the business leader, however, this important step is often overlooked or just added as an afterthought to a completed decision process. If our motivation is right—if the business is really God's and we do the business for His glory, not our own—then we are set up to pray during the decision process. We are in position to pray at every business juncture and to pray without ceasing. Yet as a practical matter, this orientation toward actively seeking God's will in prayer for business decisions often seems impossible. Things are just happening too fast.

My experience has been, however, there are very few business decisions unable to bear the delay of an earnest prayer for God's guidance. In fact, David's testimony is one of waiting on the Lord for the requested guidance.

"For You I wait all the day." From the heart after God's heart we learn to not propel ourselves, or be propelled by others, toward hasty decisions not born of careful analysis and fervent prayer. David says we should avoid haste, and as we live in God's very presence, we should "wait for the LORD; be strong and let your heart take courage; yes, wait for the LORD" (Psalm 27:14). David's saying we should not fret about the decisions before us; at the same time, we shouldn't plow ahead hastily without earnestly seeking God first and *waiting*. Our God is the sovereign God of the universe. He can change things we think we control and He can change things we can never control. It's unwise to move ahead of the God of the universe when He calls us to seek Him in prayer and wait for Him before we presumptuously act. We should wait *in faith*.

As David waited on the Lord for guidance, even though scripture may not directly apply, he still sought the Lord in the Word as he prayed. In this way David's prayers for guidance were energized by God's Word. The "enlightening of the eyes" that David spoke about in Psalm 19 often comes as we prayerfully seek the Lord for guidance in the midst of meditating on His Word. As we come to the Word in tender openness, the Holy Spirit within us speaks to our hearts to confirm a course of action or to simply give us peace to proceed with the best judgment He has given us for His business. In this process we continue to remain certain we are dwelling in His presence, seeking His glory, and leaving the results to His sovereign power and grace.

To receive the full impact of David's quest for guidance in Psalm 25, it's important that we consider the state of the heart after God's heart as he comes confidently to God for guidance. From verses 8 and 9, we understand that God guides the humble. "Good and upright is the LORD; therefore, He instructs sinners in the way. He leads the humble in justice, and He teaches the humble His way." Note the following: "He instructs sinners in the way." It doesn't say that He instructs those who are perfect (or more accurately, those who think they are perfect). "He leads the *humble*" (emphasis mine). From the rest of the psalm, we understand that the forgiven are humble and that "He teaches the *humble* His way."

The heart after God's heart tells you if you want to be led by God, you must be a humble sinner, forgiven by God as a function of His love, grace, and mercy. Anybody can do that! If you want to be led by God, you come to God in complete humility, knowing that you have access only because of His grace and without any credit to your own righteousness. So when you come to God to seek His guidance, what's the attitude of your heart? Do you come to Him with an honest attitude of contrite humility, having examined your soul, applying the blood of Christ to any and all sin, receiving His complete forgiveness? Or do you come to God with the attitude of a self-confident, self-made business leader, seeking God's blessing on your own plans?

The Word of God does not apply directly to all business situations, but when we look at David, we see a leader who gave the example of waiting before God in prayer and in faith. David knew God was present in his thoughts, and he knew God would faithfully provide guidance because the business ultimately belongs to God.

3. Business Guidance as a Result of God's Initiative, in Ways We Might Not Have Even Been Aware

As we truly walk with God, He tends to get us where we need to be. This takes us back to our discussion of acknowledging God's presence in our thoughts from the last chapter. As we embrace God's presence in each of our business thoughts, with His unconditional love, grace, mercy, power, and strength, we tend to think about different things. And as our emotions, words, and actions flow from our thoughts, we tend to find ourselves feeling, saying, and doing different things, all consistent with His loving and empowering presence in our thoughts. As the heart of David said in Psalm 143, "Let me hear Your lovingkindness in the morning; For I trust in You; teach me the way in which I should walk; for to You I lift up my soul."

In David's great psalm of confession and repentance, he put it this way: "Behold, You desire truth in the innermost being, and in the hidden part You will make me know wisdom" (Psalm 51:6). As we discussed in previous chapters, we can only have truth in our innermost being as we regularly apply the blood of Christ to our thought life. From this position of purity, we become wise in our decisions as we are very practically led by God's grace in our lives. ("In the hidden part You will make me know wisdom.")

In this way, seeking guidance in business becomes a matter of simply dwelling with God in business and receiving His grace in our thoughts. This may seem impractical, but it's actually very practical. Let's think about it. God guides us in each little moment of our lives, not just in the big moments. God's sovereign hand is always there in our lives, not just when we have a big decision. And while we know we can't possibly have a conscious awareness of God's presence in our thoughts in every moment or have pure thoughts in every moment, we *can* have this awareness of His presence in our thoughts for this moment as we apply the blood of Christ to cleanse us from any sin in our thoughts *in this moment*. And then we know we can have this same purity of thought in the next moment, as well.

If we think of a moment as a step, we can begin to tie these steps together into a "walk" with God. In each of these moments, we are faced with little decisions. For instance, decisions to think the best of an associate who said an unkind word, to see someone across the table as one whom God loves, to go out of our way to be helpful to a subordinate, to forgive an offense from the heart without being asked, to smile, to encourage, to say a kind word, to sincerely seek the best for another, to step out of someone's way, to confess lust rather than ignore it, to make the pot of coffee, to be honest in a little thing that might make you look bad, to be honestly interested in what someone is saying, to take the more difficult task, to see this as God's business rather than yours, to not seek underserved credit for little things, to give credit for the little things, to make eye contact, and so forth. We don't think about seeking God's guidance for such things. As we walk moment by moment receiving God's grace in our thought life, however, we are either obedient in all these little things or we receive God's forgiveness and complete cleansing. And then we go from there.

The accumulation of days of all these little decisions creates a direction in life. As we are either obedient or forgiven in the little things of our heart, in the accumulation of days we find ourselves on the pathway to the bigger things. It puts us in contact with certain people we might not otherwise touch. It physically moves us to a place and situation to open or close doors and be led to other aspects of God's plan for our lives and our business. This makes sense. We don't really expect for the Lord to reveal to us what we're going to do 15 years from now, but we'd like Him to show us where to go next month. Instead, God's focus is on this moment right *now*. Are we walking with Him right now? Have we honestly sought to have "truth in our innermost being" right now? That, for sure, is God's will for us right now. And from there He can lead us, as we remain obedient or forgiven in the little things of the heart in this moment, the next moment, and the next.

David says as we have "truth in the innermost being" (that is, integrity with God as He is present in our thought life), then "in the hidden part [He] will make [him] know wisdom." He makes us know Himself and His direction in ways we aren't even aware (the hidden part). It doesn't make sense that God would bypass the moment by moment, where we can recognize His presence with our thoughts, in order to show us something big way down the road—because we're not in position to receive His leading down there yet. Through this process of moment by moment walking with Him in the little things of our thoughts, however, He gets us where we need to be, and in ways we might not even recognize as it is happening. Through this process we come to "know wisdom in the hidden part."

Caution in Seeking the Counsel of Others

It is important to note that King David did not emphasize the role of counsel from others within gaining God's guidance in business. Often, in situations when we're unsure about decisions in business, we go straight to get advice from others. From what we've examined so far, we know there are things the heart after God's heart would pursue before going to others for counsel. As we've discussed, we need to seek His guidance with an honest attitude of humility, born out of sincerely recognizing our need for His grace and mercy, in order to have access to Him for guidance. We also know that in the many business situations where the general and/or specific revelation in God's Word is clear we need not go to others for counsel; we need to simply obey. Often, we go to others for counsel without first having prayed and waited on the Lord.

Business leaders tend to be people of action, and when facing important decisions, we may just go straight to others for counsel. We may be tempted to think that spending time seeking the Lord in the Word and prayerfully waiting for God to lead aren't things that will make a difference in moving us toward a decision. Or perhaps we can't imagine that the God of the universe would engage directly with us to practically lead us as He is present in our thought life. We want answers now. We'd like those answers to be audible from someone that we respect, so we can move forward now! And as a result, there is a tendency to neglect the unseen power of prayer and God's desire to guide us as we seek Him in His Word, going instead straight to ask others for advice or counsel, with all good intentions. As important as the decision may be, it's God's desire that we deepen our walk with Him through this process of seeking His guidance and thereby rely on Him more completely. This deepening relationship with God often comes through the process of earnestly seeking Him in prayer as we face important decisions. In God's economy the process is as important as the outcome; He uses the process to conform us to the image of His Son, and this *is* the outcome.

The fact is we don't see David positively speaking of the role of counselors in his business or other areas of his life anywhere in the psalms. He does, however, speak about the danger of ungodly counselors. Elsewhere in the scripture we know of the value of godly counsel. Even David's wise son, King Solomon, speaks of the value of the abundance of counselors in Proverbs 11. But we're taking our cues from the heart of King David. And the heart after God's heart, as revealed in the psalms for us, emphasizes the danger of ungodly counsel and does not even mention the value of good counsel. His warnings are so prevalent they cannot be overlooked.

Psalm 26 is a great expression of David's focus on the Lord rather than man, and his stand against those who would seek to influence him contrary to God's guidance.

> Vindicate me, O LORD, for I have walked in my integrity, and I have trusted in the LORD without wavering. Test me, O LORD, and try me; test my mind and my heart. Your lovingkindness is before my eyes, and I have walked in Your truth. I do not sit with deceitful men, nor will I go with pretenders. (Psalm 26:1–4)

David first says he has walked in humble dependence on God ("trusted in the LORD without wavering"). He goes on to say he has focused on God rather than men ("Your lovingkindness is before my eyes"), and he has obeyed the guidance God already gave him ("I have walked in Your truth"). David says he will not "sit" or go in the company of those who are involved in pretension and deceit. Recognize that for deceit to be "deceit" it has to seem right but be wrong. As you're seeking God's guidance in an area of business where God's Word is not clear—and as you're seeking to be sensitive to the voice of God—you don't want to expose yourself to the clever rationalization of those who have subtly compromised their integrity and seared their consciences over the years with "accepted business practices." It's easy to find business leaders who will reinforce an easy compromise if your heart is already seeking to justify or assuage your own conscience in a matter.

David goes on in Psalm 26:8, bringing us back to a focus on living in the very presence of God almighty ("the place where Your glory dwells"). From here we are in an easy position to be led by God. From here we must be conscious of *avoiding* the influence of those that are not living in the presence of God. David says, "Do not take my soul away along with sinners" (verse 9). We're all vulnerable to falling into sin. Left to ourselves in business, we are prone to develop schemes not entirely honest or to seek unfair influence. Those to whom we would go to for counsel are subject to the same temptations. According to David, we are to avoid those who have fallen to "a wicked scheme, and whose right hand is full of bribes" (verse 10). David warns us to be very careful about going along with those who have been deceived in this way. ("Do not take my soul away along with sinners.") This brings us back to focusing on our own hearts and maintaining our own purity. Only by continuing to come back to the Lord to have our hearts made pure by the blood of Jesus are we able to stay in the place where God's glory dwells—in His very presence. From here, God leads us.

I was the CEO of a public company that was also a Christian company. Although the company's stock was publicly traded, the company had a Christian mission that was included in its articles of incorporation and all the employees were committed Christian people. We did business most often with Christian organizations and most of our customers were Christians. Yet one of the most sobering aspects in leading this company was the progressive realization that so many of these vaunted "ministry businesses" were engaged in deceit and pretension. Many of these ministries' methods of business were compromised even while seeking to fulfill an inspired mission. On one occasion, a Christian organization—in the midst of a conversation about a potential advertising campaign—accidentally did not "mute" themselves during a call and revealed to us their corporate heart with deceit and manipulation associated with everything they had just presented to us. Looking back though, I realize that I had also become so focused on succeeding in the "mission" that I often overlooked the fundamental issues of walking with God as I sought to accomplish His mission. The business had subtly become something that I was going to succeed at, rather than a work of God. And this was a totally Christian business, with Christian employees, customers, and partners. How much greater is the temptation in secular business? All this is to emphasize the challenge of obtaining godly business counsel. It's easy to find a counselor who will happily agree with your rationalization of a situation. Even though David had access to any one of God's people as the King of Israel, we see in his psalms an intensity to go to God for guidance and a caution in going to others.

So as you consider the idea of seeking the counsel of others, the core of David's exhortation to you is to be very careful that you are continuing to walk with God, confident in His presence and His desire to directly lead you, consistent with His sovereignty and love. Make sure you're seeking godly counsel from this place and not short-circuiting the process of seeking God's heart. Certainly, we do not go to the "wicked who prosper." David had a heart after God's heart. He did not have a heart after man's heart.

Yet there are godly people who through years of study and application have come to know the scripture better. Those people can help you become aware of the general and/or specific revelation of God in His Word, which has direct application to your business situation. Mature Christians, and especially mature Christian business leaders, can be helpful in exposing relevant scripture to your business decisions. As we've already discussed in applying the heart of King David, God's guidance in business is first found in applying His clear revelation through His Word to our business. So we should make it clear should we go for counsel that we are seeking our counselor's help in understanding the application of specific scripture to our situation. Tell them how you have been seeking the Lord in prayer and how He has been working in your heart as you've waited for Him. This will help you and your counselor separate the opinion and rationalizations of man from the Word of God and the leading of His Spirit.

Guidance in Business Planning

I do a lot of strategic business planning. God uses the gifts He has given me in this area to help companies exercise dominion over God's creation and to provide for my family. The very nature of strategic planning requires the Christian leader to actively seek God's guidance. Strategic planning is a business function that combines all the elements David specifies in seeking and receiving God's guidance in business.

As we approach the strategic process, let's first check our motivation. "For You are my rock and my fortress; for Your name's sake You will lead me and guide me" (Psalm 31:3). Am I seeking God's guidance in this business plan for His name's sake—for His glory? Or is it all about me and I'm really just hoping God will help me do a little better in it? As a practical matter, my experience is that business plans that are driven by a leader's ego are flawed plans.

In going through the mechanics of developing the plan, we prayerfully apply the Word of God to each aspect. Simply applying the Word of God to our plan takes many potential business alternatives off the table. And the heart after God's heart tells us that the Word of God "enlightens our eyes." My testimony is as I go to the Word in the context of business planning, the Lord does indeed provide very practical insights in defining attitudes, more productive courses of action, and improved methods of motivation and management. As we plan and move consistent with the Word of God, our faith in Him gives us confidence in the direction He has provided, knowing that in keeping His Word "there is great reward." This helps produce conviction and motivational enthusiasm from the Lord, through us, to our people as we communicate our business direction.

I've heard it said that planning without praying produces a plan without a prayer. Since the business is the Lord's and not ours, we can't possibly develop a plan for His business without earnestly seeking Him in prayer. If we're honest with ourselves, we're sometimes tempted to think of praying as a legalistic waste of time but necessary in order to feel good about our plans. The reality is that the God of creation wants us to seek Him in prayer as we plan. Through this prayer He provides the insights needed to plan His business, and He also draws our heart to Himself in the midst of this important process. We must give planning the time it needs, because an integral part of planning is praying and *waiting*. Business planning, done right, requires significant, dedicated time. So often leaders try to fit this into small windows, which really don't give the time needed, just to get the plan done without even thinking about praying and waiting. David's example in his business planning is best summarized in Psalm 25:4–5. "Make me know Your ways, O LORD; teach me Your paths. Lead me in Your truth and teach me … for You I wait all the day."

Finally, when planning is a function that must be performed today, we must walk with God moment by moment through today's planning process. We plan from the strength and stability of being in the very presence of God almighty. And as we walk with Him through today's planning tasks, we move forward in confidence that the Lord will make the heart after God's heart "know wisdom in the hidden part."

Confidence in God's Business Guidance

> Delight yourself in the Lord; and He will give you the desires
> of your heart. Commit your way to the Lord, trust also in
> Him, and he will do it. He will bring forth your righteousness
> as the light and your judgment as the noonday. Rest in the
> LORD and wait patiently for Him. (Psalm 37:4–7)

The business leader who, like David, has made his business God's business, who has sought God in His Word and prayerfully waited for His leading, and who is embracing God's presence in his thoughts as he walks with Him should have faith that God is leading at the time when it is required for him to make the necessary judgments.

Part of a moment-by-moment walk with God is seeing Him engage in thoughts, words, and actions to bless and enable the gifts that He has given you. Another part of this walk is seeing your desires joyously transformed to align with God's will. And finally, part of this walk is seeing Him transform your own judgment and make you wise in business—wisdom in the hidden part.

The Christian business leader who is walking with God should be confident that God's grace is leading even in areas where He hasn't shouted His will from the heavens. Because you are certain that you will be led by God as you walk with Him, you can praise and thank God for leading that you have not yet received with no less certainty than you thank God for guidance already received. When you have real faith in the leading of God almighty you will have confidence in the direction of your business leadership, which is founded on God and not yourself. This is the powerful position of King David and it's a key component of a heart after God's heart—and developing *Business after God's Heart.*

CHAPTER 6

Business Trials and Business Cycles

Blessed be the Lord, for He
has made marvelous His
lovingkindness to me in a besieged city.
—Psalm 31:21

Call Them Trials

David certainly had his share of trials in the business God gave him to lead. And if you are a business leader, most of the trials in your life will be business trials. I can say this with confidence simply because of the sheer weight of time spent at work. In addition to this, as a business leader you must accomplish objectives that are simply not easy. You must "subdue the earth," the world's system, or just plain entropy that resists your exercise of dominion. Adversity is something to be overcome almost every day, whether it's difficult employees, demanding bosses, unreasonable clients, or failing equipment.

As business leaders, if we don't recognize our spiritual trials at work, then we will fail to apply faith in the Word of God to the primary arena for trials in our lives. Despite this fact, we seldom call business trials "spiritual trials." Instead, we like to refer to them as "challenges," "issues," or "situations." It's easy to get swept up in the lexicon of the world, especially because effectively communicating with unbelieving colleagues is essential in business. And so we are together involved in "challenges" that should be very clearly for us "spiritual trials."

Years ago, I helped a dear friend and entrepreneur strategically position his growing software company. One day he came to the board, where I also engaged, needing counsel for a very substantial conflict. His successful company had recently been acquired by a large public company and he had remained with the business to try to make the combination successful. He spoke openly with us about the extreme problems he was encountering in dealing with the parent company and the resulting consequences for his staff and his clients. He sought advice for the best approach to integrate his business into the parent for higher performance and particularly for dealing with the executives in authority over his subsidiary.

It was obvious after he described the tale of woe, so often associated with integrating an acquisition, that my friend was at the end of his rope and was seeking our counsel on the way out of an extremely difficult predicament. The first thing one distinguished board member told him had nothing whatsoever to do with the substantive predicament just described. Instead he told my friend to avoid referring to the difficulties as a "problem." "Call it a 'situation' or an 'opportunity,'" he said, "but not a 'problem.' People don't want to hear about problems, and you certainly don't want to be associated with a 'problem.'"

While relabeling things can sometimes be helpful for business politics, as Christian businesspeople we have bought into this relabeling of things in ways that can hinder us from applying the Word of God to our hearts. When we come home from work talking about having a tough day or someone making life difficult for us, we allow our focus to shift off applying God's Word to the *spiritual trials* we face. So for right now, let's consider our challenges, problems, opportunities, issues, and situations in our business as our spiritual trials, and let's see what the Lord has for our souls as we look to the example of the heart after God's heart.

Expect Business Trials

Our hero, David, certainly had trials. Because he recognized his "business" was God's business, he spoke openly to God about his business trials (a good lesson for us). Psalm 55 is just one example from David as he expressed his heart to the One who he knew would save him in the midst of his trials.

Give ear to my prayer, O God; and do not hide Yourself from my supplication. Give heed to me and answer me; I am restless in my complaint and am surely distracted ... My heart is in anguish within me and the terrors of death have fallen upon me. Fear and trembling come upon me, horror has overwhelmed me ... For it is not an enemy who reproaches me, then I could bear it; nor is it one who hates me who has exalted himself against me, then I could hide myself from him. But it is you, a man my equal, my companion and my familiar friend; we who had sweet fellowship together walked in the house of God in the throng ... As for me, I shall call upon God, and the LORD will save me ... Cast your burden upon the LORD and He will sustain you; He will never allow the righteous to be shaken. (Psalm 55:1–3, 4–5, 12–14, 16, 22)

Notice here that while David had faith in God to deliver him from his trial, the trial was still very real. David didn't get a free pass. The language in this psalm clearly expresses the magnitude of the trial and the intensity of David's feeling in the midst of it all. He says, "My heart is in anguish within me." Those are not cheap words. His heart really was in anguish. He was going through a great trial with those he worked with and with those he competed against. Things were not going as planned—they were not going as he would like for them to go—so much so that he was in anguish. How much anguish? So much that "the terrors of death [had] fallen upon [him]" and his fear was so great that he was physically trembling and "horror [had] overwhelmed [him]." This anguish, this fear, and this trembling are expressed from the heart that is called the heart after God's heart. This heart endured real trials, and so shall we.

Expect to have trials in business. Embracing this expectation has the effect of preparing us for trials. As Peter says, "Beloved, do not be surprised at the fiery ordeal among you, which comes upon you for your testing, as though some strange thing were happening to you" (1 Peter 4:12). By cultivating faith that we will have trials in business, just as David did, we are prepared to call them trials when they occur and avoid the crisis of surprise, "as though some strange thing were happening to you." A surprised and bewildered business leader is an ineffective business leader.

God Uses Trials to Shape David's Heart (and Ours Too)

We should also expect God to minister deeply to our souls during the expected business trial. David expresses God's ministry through trials in this way: "Blessed be the LORD, for He has made marvelous His lovingkindness to me in a besieged city" (Psalm 31:21). Notice David is praising God for His ministry to his soul in the time of trial. Let's face it. If you are holed up in a besieged city, you are in a major trial. This really happened to David. He was holding out in a city that was surrounded and under siege. This was a huge trial that related primarily to David's "business." He was responsible not just for his own life but for all those who were with him. He was responsible for having gotten them into the trial in the first place and then for providing for their sustenance and defense. The magnitude of this business trial could easily overwhelm anyone. In fact, this feeling of being overwhelmed is part of the psychology apply by those who are laying siege. In the midst of this, God did a great work in David's heart. David does not tell us that God lifted the siege. Rather, he tells us the important thing God did was having "made marvelous His lovingkindness to me." God used the trial to make His love marvelous to David. It's not that God changed the love He had for David during the siege. It's that God used the trial in David's life to give David a clearer view of the reality and the character of His love. And to be certain of the personal, infinite, and unconditional love of the God of the universe is a marvelous blessing!

While we can easily know what the Bible says about the reality and character of God's love for us, it can take something more to apply faith that is as good as sight in the reality and character of this personal love for us. David saw that God used this extreme trial to give him something extremely valuable: a true personal experience of God's marvelous love. Like David, we should expect God to do great works in our own hearts in and through the trials that He permits in our business. James famously tells us, "Consider it all joy, my brethren, when you encounter various trials, knowing that the testing of your faith produces endurance. And let endurance have its perfect result, so that you may be perfect and complete, lacking in nothing" (James 1:2–4). Our faith in His plan to use trials in this way should be so real that we actually have joy, like James says, even in the midst of the trial. This is the reason why a Christian business leader can honestly smile while not panicking in times of trial. This is the reason why you can have real serenity when others are distraught. This is why you can steer a steady course while calmly reacting to adversity. And this is why you can look beyond the focus of the trial to the people who are enduring the trial and seize the opportunity to minister to their hearts while also guiding the business.

David's Perspective on the Brevity of Trials Shaped His Heart

"Into Your hands I commit My spirit" (Luke 23:46). These words of Christ that He spoke as He hung on the cross, in the midst of His greatest trial, were the exact words that David prophetically spoke as he endured the trials chronicled in Psalm 31. From the heart of David and the life of Christ we gain a perspective that trials are generally short, relative to the scheme of life and eternity. Jesus spoke, "Into Your hands I commit My spirit" only a few moments before He would spend eternity with the Father to whom He spoke. His time left on earth—His time of trial—was indeed short when compared to an eternity of bliss in the presence of His Father, which He experienced before and after His time on earth.

Jesus's focus on the eternity with the Father, which He spoke of on the cross, was reinforced by the Spirit in Hebrews 12:1–2. Here we are encouraged to follow Jesus's example in maintaining an eternal perspective during trials. "And let us run with endurance the race that is set before us, fixing our eyes on Jesus, the author and perfecter of faith, who for the joy set before Him endured the cross, despising the shame, and has sat down at the right hand of the throne of God." Jesus looked ahead to the "joy set before Him" in the midst of the trial and the shame. And David's identification with Christ as he faced his trial in Psalm 31 is also an example to us during our trials. His words stand as an encouragement to us to identify with Christ and maintain an eye for eternity with the Father as we endure our times of trial here. As David and Christ said, our souls are in the hands of our Father for eternity. This is a very long time. Real faith in this eternally long time without trials should sustain us in the relatively brief time of trial; despite however long the trial may seem, it is temporal, and the relief from trial is eternal.

Yet for most business leaders, the length of even our longest trials is relatively short. David expressed this "short bad/long good" mentality in Psalm 30:5 when he said, "For His anger is but for a moment, His favor is for a lifetime; Weeping may last for the night, but a shout of joy comes in the morning." From this we see that God does permit or even cause business trials, but He does keep them relatively brief. Sometimes we're tempted to think that trials will never end, but this is simply wrong. During the deepest trials in business we must recognize, from the Word of God and our own experience, the trial will end relatively soon, and relatively soon we will look back on the trial as a low point already well behind us. If our perspective becomes distorted, and we subconsciously feel like our business trial is endless, it's easy to fall into despair and make bad business decisions. The effect of this kind of leadership will, in turn, exacerbate the trial that started it all.

In the deepest trials as CEO of Crosswalk.com, there were days I lost my perspective, gave in to despair, and failed in my leadership. I can remember feeling totally weighed down as I considered more and more bad news from the market; every alternative tactic to recover the business was progressively smashed, and I lived with the knowledge of having to lay off still more dear, talented brothers and sisters in Christ whom I had attracted to the business. In the flesh, this trial seemed endless. I was in no position to be effective in leadership with such a state of mind. Only when I looked to the Lord and gained His perspective on the relative brevity of the trial was I able to be effective. And beyond this, with these trials very far behind me, God has taken me beyond faith to sight in knowing that all these business trials indeed pass. He has taught me the really important thing is the *way* I endure the trial.

Learn to Recognize the Highs and Lows

David recognized that trials have a cyclical nature. As businesspeople we recognize that the economy goes through cycles. We also recognize most businesses are subjected to the ups and downs driven by the overall economy and seasonality, or simply from the ebb and flow of successes and failures. Just as we know there are cycles in business, we need to understand that there are cycles in business trials. And our expectation of cycles of spiritual trials in business leadership should be even more certain than our expectation of economic and business cycles.

The reaction of David's heart to the highs and lows brought about by his trials is vividly captured in his psalms. He knows that God will see him through the cycles of trials, minister to his soul, and ultimately give him God's perspective on the trial. Psalm 30 not only expresses the relative brevity of trials as we discussed, but it also expresses well the ups and downs David faced during his cycle of trials as he summarized in verses 4 and 5. "Sing praise to the LORD, you His godly ones, And give thanks to His holy name. For His anger is but for a moment, His favor is for a lifetime; Weeping may last for the night, But a shout of joy comes in the morning."

In this great psalm, David goes on to share his heart that's cycling up in verse 6 and the beginning of verse 7. "Now as for me, I said in my prosperity, 'I will never be moved.' O LORD, by Your favor You have made my mountain to stand strong." Then he's looking into a down cycle by the end of verse 7 and through verse 10. "You hid Your face, I was dismayed. To You, O LORD, I called, and to the Lord I made supplication: 'What profit is there in my blood, if I go down to the pit? Will the dust praise You? Will it declare Your faithfulness? 'Hear, O LORD, and be gracious to me; O LORD, be my helper.'" Ending on a high and optimistic note, as the expressions of David's heart normally do, here are verses 11 and 12. "You have turned for me my mourning into dancing; You have loosed my sackcloth and girded me with gladness, that my soul may sing praise to You and not be silent. O LORD my God, I will give thanks to You forever."

You can probably identify with the cycles of trials that David expressed in Psalm 30. Life's ups and downs are experienced by each of us more vividly than the cycles in businesses that are studied by economists. In God's economy, trial cycles are a fact of life.

David understood these cycles and, more importantly, when he experienced these cycles of trials, he applied faith in God's goodness and His purpose for the trial, even as he maintained a perspective on the cyclical nature of his experience. Looking at David, we see a life characterized by extreme cycles that shaped his heart and generated his psalms. He was faithful in the little he had as a boy, in obscurity tending sheep; he was chosen by God and anointed by Samuel the priest; he was a hero of Israel defeating Goliath; he was a fugitive running from King Saul; he was skilled in tactics and effective in evading and battling Saul; he was made king; he sinned in business; he sinned in his personal life; he sinned in enormous ways beyond anything imaginable for a man of God; he lived in misery; he was broken and forgiven; he was restored spiritually; his kingdom was restored; he was given a wise son to succeed him; centuries later he was called a man after God's heart. David's life was not lived on the mountaintop of victory. His was a life of victories and defeats, even devastating defeats, the Lord used to shape a heart of dependence. David was a man who endured the cycles of trials just as we do.

Reflecting on Life Brings the Perspective of Trials' Cyclical Nature

I experienced the time compression of the cycle of trials during the wild days of internet business from 1998 to 2001. At that time, many said that "internet time" was much faster than regular time and that a single year on the internet was like seven years in the real world. I like to say I aged on internet time, which is like aging in dog years. Each year certainly felt like seven years of experience—and aging! Everything was compressed into an extremely high-speed exercise featuring a high-amplitude, high-frequency adventure in business cycles, and spiritual trials.

You'll remember from chapter 3 that we began with a very small office, small staff, little capital, no product, and no revenues. Then nine months later, we branded our business/ministry as Crosswalk.com. Soon we were the largest Christian presence on the internet, I had been on CNBC twice, we had feature articles in *USA Today* and *Money Magazine,* and we had huge traffic on our web site and were ranked by Nielsen Net Ratings as one of the top sites in the world! Our stock was soaring, and we were mentioned by Tom Brokaw as one of the high-flying stocks of the internet on *NBC Nightly News.* A few months later, our stock settled back to internet reality, such as it was, and shortly thereafter we had technical difficulties as the traffic swamped our technical infrastructure. We recovered, as did our stock, but before we could catch our breath, several determined and well-financed competitors chased us in the market and took market share. As we recovered from this by setting a strategy to move the company toward a positive cash-flow and assured survival, regardless of the competitive landscape, the internet sector of the stock market began to slide into what would a little later become a total internet market collapse (what I like to remember as "dot-bomb"). During this slide, I had to lead through the agony of massive layoffs and a devastating business environment with no hope of real recovery. Incredibly, this entire saga was all compressed into two years and eight months!

This wasn't the end of the story though (or the end of the cycles). In one of the lowest of the lows, as I departed Crosswalk, God made His love marvelous to me too. He did an amazing work to deepen my understanding of His love for me and to give me a perspective on His engagement in business. My business low became my spiritual high. In fact, today my perspective is different, mainly as a result of studying David's heart. Today, I look back and see the cycles of my life, which gives me perspective as I look ahead and experience both the ups and downs that should be expected as I walk with God, consistent with His plan, His faithfulness, His love, and His economy. And hopefully He's also using me to help others gain His perspective on the trials each day in business.

Looking back on your own life will help give perspective on the cycles of trials you are yet to experience. If you take the time to chart the experiences of your life, particularly the real highs and lows that shaped who you are, you will gain a better understanding of yourself along with a pattern of trials. This understanding will help you interpret and endure current and future trials. You will see a pattern of God's faithfulness and will recognize that each of these trials has passed, as your current trial is bound to pass, just as David recognized.

Jim Buick, a good friend and former chairman of the Crosswalk.com board of directors (and former CEO of Zondervan), helped me gain this perspective while I was studying David's psalms. After I left Crosswalk, Jim invited me to spend a few days at his home where he helped me develop what he referred to as a "life plan." During this process, he helped me chart my entire life on a very large roll of paper. The discipline of getting through this over the course of a couple of days of deep reflection was extremely valuable in systematically looking back on the cycles of trials and the way

God used the trials to very positively build His character into my life and to direct me through the important junctures in my life. I've encouraged many to undertake this exercise and without exception, the Lord has used it to provide insight into their strengths, weaknesses, vulnerabilities, and particularly into God's faithfulness in trials. Understanding the cyclical nature of God's economy from David's psalms and the overall counsel of scripture, together with an understanding of the specific cycles of your own experience, help form a foundation to interpret and endure business trials that lie ahead.

David Endured Trials from the "Zone"

The *heart after God's heart* found a place from which to lead those entrusted to his care which he describes in various ways. For David this place is "under His wings," it's a "rock," it's a "fortress," it's a "refuge," it's a "tower," and it's a "shield." All these are rhetorical references to the same place, which we will call the "Zone." David found this Zone through a life of trials, defeats, and victories. It is tested and true. It's a Zone of the heart and not a physical place. The heart of David, the *heart after God's heart,* leads from this "Zone," especially in times of trial. It's a position of total security, stability, and confidence. We will look at several of these pictures independently, but we must recognize that it's not just one independent picture. The Zone represents the combined meaning of all the pictures David gives us to experience as we have active faith in God's character and His care for us.

First, the Zone is in *the shadow of God's wings.* What a picture! See yourself right now leading your business in the very shadow of the "wings" of almighty God. David's certainty that he was in the shadow of the wings of almighty God so affected him that he sang for joy. "When I remember You on my bed, I meditate on You in the night watches, for You have been my help, and in the shadow of Your wings I sing for joy" (Psalm 63:6–7). David was not just on his bed. Through his eyes of faith, David could see he personally was in the shadow of the wings of the God of the universe. In your times of trial, as you lie sleeplessly on your bed, through your eyes of faith see yourself under the wings of God almighty. As David said in Psalm 91, "He will cover you with His pinions [or soft feathers]." This is a place of security and tenderness, close to the heart of God, which is given as a gift of His grace even in the midst of business threats.

Next, the Zone is on *the Rock*. In Psalm 18:31 David tells us that God is *the* Rock. "For who is God, but the LORD? And who is a rock, except our God?" Later in verse 46, David says the Lord is "*my* rock." "The LORD lives, and blessed be my rock; And exalted be the God of my salvation." The picture of a rock communicates stability and strength. In Psalm 31 and Psalm 62, David says that the Lord is the rock of David's strength. God's strength has replaced David's weakness, and from this position of God's strength, David is able to effectively rule. If you apply this picture to business, the Rock represents a solid base from which to operate business, rather than the shifting sand of your own wits, your company's business processes, or your boss's brilliance. Your soul is to rest upon the Rock as you lead your business. Business built on the Rock within you will be a stable business. The business will not be immune from difficulties and trials, but you will have a stable base from which to deal with these trials.

The Zone is *a Fortress*. In Psalm 31:1 David connects the image of the rock with that of the fortress as he prays, "For You are my rock and my fortress ..." The fortress is on the rock. This picture the Holy Spirit has for us is both stable and protected in uncertain and threatening times. And notice that David said that the Lord is "my fortress." The image here is of God as David's *personal* fortress. God is his intimate fortress—a fortress for his heart. This perfect fortress exists for the business leader at the point of trial, just as it existed for David. The heart after God's heart is certain this unassailable fortress surrounds it, which is God Himself. This heart is totally protected; it is completely safe. Take a moment and visualize the core of who you are—the beginning of where your thoughts come from (your heart)—being completely surrounded and protected by God almighty like an impregnable fortress. From this spot, this Zone, you lead your business.

The Zone is also *a Refuge*. "For you have been my stronghold and a refuge in the day of my distress" (Psalm 59:16). In our cycles of trials, we know we will all have "the day of my distress." On that day, the heart after God's heart says, "God is my refuge." The picture David gives us here is of a place of safety and resort when threatened as a result of things we have done or errors we have made. This harkens back to the concept of cities of refuge that were established by Old Testament Law. These cities of refuge were strategically placed around Israel for the innocent who accidentally killed another. The feeling a person would have after accidentally killing someone is not unlike the feeling of a business leader whose business is failing because of his mistakes or through no fault of his own. David, learning much from his times of distress, gives us an extremely valuable picture of the refuge his heart found during those times. "How great is Your goodness, which You have stored up for those who fear You, which You have wrought for those who take refuge in You, before the sons of men! You hide them in the secret place of Your presence from the conspiracies of man; You keep them secretly in a shelter from the strife of tongues" (Psalm 31:19–20). In business distress, David exhorts your heart to faith that God's goodness is stored for you in the secret place of His presence. Be certain that God Himself has protected your heart from the strife and even the conspiracies. And from this Zone of God's refuge, you will remain clearheaded and confident at the core of your being, making you more effective in leading God's business.

The Zone is *a Tower*. It's time to get some height into the Zone! "For You have been a refuge for me, a tower of strength against the enemy" (Psalm 61:3). In David's day they built towers to watch over pastures, vineyards, or cities. The purpose was to see into the distance and warn of coming threats. In a fortress the tower is also usually the strongest point of defense. With God as your tower, you can rest confident you will see what God would have you see of the coming business threats. You need not worry you will be overtaken by some strange ordeal beyond the sovereign power of the God of the universe who loves you infinitely. The business leader can be paralyzed by the unknown. You can live in fear of the unknown in a way that hurts the ongoing operations of business. Those being led can feel this vibe coming from the leader who is so affected. David here inspires your faith in the God who is your tower. This picture supports optimism and confidence that God will give you visibility and strength to prepare for and deal with unknown threats yet to surface.

Lastly, the Zone is *Behind the Shield*. "But You, O Lord, are a shield about me, my glory and the One who lifts my head" (Psalm 3:3). Here we see David had a pretty high-tech vision for the shield that defends the Zone, saying that the Lord is "a shield about me." This shield for the heart after God's heart is a shield that *surrounds* the Zone. To use a traditional shield effectively, you must be alert and hold it in the direction of the threat. The picture of God's shield is not like that. He is not just protecting you when you're paying attention and when you understand the threat. He's protecting you twenty-four/seven and from every threat—even those you had never anticipated. This picture also shows His protection when the threats are very close to your heart. When a shield is engaged in combat, it's a life-or-death struggle with the flow of adrenaline, sweat, wounds, blood, terror, and exhaustion. There are times in business when it seems you're living your business life in a panic of thrusts and parries that are consuming every ounce of your energy, wits, and resourcefulness. In those moments, when the trials are very personal and immediate, you must recognize you live behind God's shield as you are settled in the Zone of His protection. Even in the midst of close combat, God brings peace to your soul and greater effectiveness in your leadership.

Practical Help for Enduring Trials

Beyond leading from the "Zone," the heart after God's heart also guides us toward practical things to do and perspectives to have when we find ourselves in times of business trial. These have been summarized below into ten guidelines, which can be used to help you systematically examine your heart and reinforce the encouragement of David in the expected business trials.

David's Ten Guidelines for Trials

1. Rejoice in the expected trial. The heart after God's heart endured unending waves of trials; we should expect nothing less as we also lead in His business. David was a great man of God and a great leader, and his life was characterized by a sequence of severe trials God used to shape and guide him to become the man after His own heart. So welcome the expected trial with joy as you walk with the author and perfecter of your faith. Expect Him to bless you as He did David in David's time of siege. "Blessed be the LORD, for He has made marvelous His lovingkindness to me in a besieged city" (Psalm 31:21).

If you are caught by surprise at first, recognize the trial as something you should have been expecting. "Beloved, do not be surprised at the fiery ordeal among you, which comes upon you for your testing, as though some strange thing were happening to you" (1 Peter 4:12). And as you walk with God, expect Him to put His joy in your heart even in the midst of the trial. "Consider it all joy, my brethren, when you encounter various trials …" (James 1:2). Know that joy is a fruit of the Spirit, and if His joy is not there even in times of trial, examine your heart to ensure you are in the position of the righteous. This leads us to the second guideline.

2. Examine your heart for sin. Because we are easily deceived and because God is faithful, He uses trials to get our attention, as He did with David in Psalm 32:3–5.

> When I kept silent about my sin, my body wasted away through my groaning all day long. For day and night Your hand was heavy upon me; My vitality was drained away as with the fever heat of summer. I acknowledged my sin to You, And my iniquity I did not hide; I said, "I will confess my transgressions to the LORD;" And You forgave the guilt of my sin.

Here we see when our hero was silent about his sin, the Lord sent a trial to get his attention.

David says, "How blessed is he whose transgression is forgiven, whose sin is covered! How blessed is the man to whom the LORD does not impute iniquity, and in whose spirit there is no deceit" (Psalm 32:1–2). This is where we want to be. Because we know one reason the Lord may permit trials is to reveal sin, we need to examine ourselves whenever we find ourselves in times of business trial to make sure sin is dealt with by the blood of Christ. The Lord encourages us to systematically examine our hearts for sin on a regular basis, as well as when we take communion, *and* in times of trial.

So when we find ourselves in times of trial, we should pray Psalm 139:23–24, just as David did. "Search me, O God, and know my heart; Try me and know my anxious thoughts; And see if there be any hurtful way in me, And lead me in the everlasting way." Having received God's mercy and grace in forgiveness and complete cleansing, we know from this point on we are in the position of the righteous. From this position of complete purity (even if the trial may have been originally caused by our sin), we endure the trial in His presence, accessing His power, and receiving the supernatural spiritual strength that only He can provide.

3. Examine your business for sin. God can use trials in business to reveal sin in the life of the business leader and to reveal sin in the business. In David's case, he was the leader of the entire enterprise and was responsible to seek God's cleansing of his own life; since the business was all within David's authority, he could examine the enterprise and correct any areas of corporate sin. Business owners and CEOs have this kind of broad authority and responsibility as an extension of their own walk with God. In times of business trial, the business leader can and should examine the area over which you have responsibility and authority for any "business sins" the Lord would have you correct. It's healthy to periodically and systematically scan your business for areas of deception, dishonesty, or unfairness with customers, employees, or business partners. And lovingly correcting wrongs that have been left to fester will help create an environment of active care and honor that can be contagious as God Himself improves the culture of your business, by His grace. In times of business trial, you may even consider inviting those in your area of responsibility to participate with you. Recently, I led an "Honor Up Stand Down" for one of my clients during which each manager was encouraged to systematically examine their area of responsibility for any dishonoring practices and were led to make positive changes.

4. Maintain a short bad/long good perspective. In the midst of trial, we should remind ourselves what we learned from the heart of David that most trials have a relatively short term. We should cultivate an expectation that the current trial will soon end. David said, "Weeping may last for the night, but a shout of joy comes in the morning" (Psalm 30:5). While we understand this from David's experience, we can also understand it from our own experience in business. When you find yourself in a time of trial, take a moment to consciously look back over your business life and see all the trials that seemed so huge and lengthy at the time are well behind you. Further, recognize God uses trials to help you develop and maintain an eternal perspective.

5. Pray in faith. In David's trials, he prayed. He prayed *a lot.* And so should we. In times of business trial, as business leaders, we are wired to do a lot of things to try to quickly squirm out of our predicament. We are not so wired, however, to pray—to pray a lot. We ought to pray a lot in our times of business trial. In Psalm 6 we see David's example of a prayer of faith in the midst of trial.

> Be gracious to me, O Lord, for I am pining away; heal me, O Lord, for my bones are dismayed. And my soul is greatly dismayed; but You, O Lord—how long? Return, O Lord, rescue my soul; save me because of Your lovingkindness … Depart from me, all you who do iniquity, for the Lord has heard the voice of my weeping. The Lord has heard my supplication; the Lord receives my prayer. (Psalm 6:2–4, 8–9)

Notice David, in communion with the Lord, is open about his trial and the condition of his heart. He is not, however, just using his wits to exit the trial; he is appealing to the God of the universe who is able to provide the needed help. And he has put real faith in God's answer to his prayer. In times of trial, we need to pour out our hearts to God and pray in faith for His will. A prayer offered in real faith can only come from a settled heart.

6. Wait in faith. Waiting is not something with which many in business are comfortable. Yet through trials, God is doing work in our hearts, and often that work can only really be done over time. Endurance is not developed in a short sprint but in a long run. "When you encounter various trials, know that the testing of your faith produces endurance. And let endurance have its perfect result, so that you may be perfect and complete, lacking in nothing" (James 1:2–4).

David resisted the temptation to put confidence in his flesh to remove his trial and set an example for the heart that waits on the Lord's deliverance in Psalm 40:1–4 (emphasis mine).

> *I waited patiently for the* LORD; and He inclined to me and heard my cry. He brought me up out of the pit of destruction, out of the miry clay, and He set my feet upon a rock making my footsteps firm. He put a new song in my mouth, a song of praise to our God; many will see and fear and will trust in the LORD. How blessed is the man who has made the LORD his trust, And has not turned to the proud, nor to those who lapse into falsehood.

Not only is David's heart settled as he waits on the Lord, but when the Lord works through the trial to do His work, it stands as a testimony to those who have been observing David's trial. Because we all go through trials in the workplace, the manner of our transit through the trials is observed by those around us. By waiting in faith on the Lord in our time of trial, we become a living testimony to God's greatness experienced by a soul whose life is fully His.

7. Do not fret. Fretting, or worrying, should be a red flag telling you that something is wrong in the way that you are enduring your business trial. Our existence in business may be so characterized by the perpetual presence of worry that we don't even recognize it as a problem. When you wait in faith, however, you do not worry. The Holy Spirit speaks eloquent words of encouragement to us through David in Psalm 37; allow them to minister to your soul.

> *Do not fret* because of evildoers, be not envious toward wrongdoers … Rest in the LORD and wait patiently for Him; *do not fret* because of him who prospers in his way, because of the man who carries out wicked schemes. Cease from anger and forsake wrath; *do not fret*; it leads only to evildoing … And you will look carefully for his place and he will not be there. But the humble will inherit the land and will delight themselves in abundant prosperity. (Psalm 37:1, 7–8, 11; emphasis mine)

The Word of God through David is very clear. *"Do Not Worry!"* In the midst of an extreme trial, threatening the survival of our business, we're told, "Do not worry." In fact, Psalm 37 says in the midst of this kind of test, worry "leads to evildoing" (verse 8). Nobody relates business worries to evildoing—nobody, that is, except the Holy Spirit through the words of a great leader and man of God. So in business trials, when the red flag of worry tells you something is wrong in your heart, follow David's example. Consciously apply your faith to your knowledge of your trustworthy God, and wait in confidence for His awesome abundance for your soul, even in the midst of business trials.

8. *Awaken praise and thanksgiving.* Praise and thanksgiving should flow from our hearts even in the midst of trials. The example flowing from the heart of David in Psalm 57 is exactly this. David is fleeing for his life, from the pursuit of Saul and his army. Take a moment and put yourself in David's position. A powerful man, whom you served diligently, has turned against you and is using his overpowering force to seek and kill you and all those under your authority. The unfairness and intensity of David's trial is beyond any you are likely to encounter in your business. Your heart is pounding; you don't have any good choices; the trial is beyond threatening just your business's survival; death is, in fact, a distinct possibility and perhaps even a probability. In this predicament, David pours out his heart to God.

> My soul is among lions; I must lie among those who breathe forth fire, even the sons of men, whose teeth are spears and arrows and their tongue a sharp sword. Be exalted above the heavens, O God; let Your glory be above all the earth. They have prepared a net for my steps; my soul is bowed down; they dug a pit before me; they themselves have fallen into the midst of it. (Selah.) My heart is steadfast, O God, my heart is steadfast; I will sing, yes, I will sing praises! Awake, my glory! Awake, harp and lyre! I will awaken the dawn. I will give thanks to You, O Lord, among the peoples; I will sing praises to You among the nations. For Your lovingkindness is great to the heavens and Your truth to the clouds. Be exalted above the heavens, O God; let Your glory be above all the earth. (Psalm 57:4–11)

The heart after God's heart doesn't necessarily give praise and thanksgiving at the initiation of the trial, but as he recognizes his condition openly with God ("my soul is bowed down"), he tells himself to "wake up and smell the glory!"

In a severe trial, David's example is to remind us that God's personal love for us is beyond all measure (to the heavens). With this reminder, we "awaken" praise. This praise is not because the trial is removed but because of a certainty of faith that the sovereign God of the universe will use this trial in our lives consistent with His infinite, unconditional love for us. Sincere praise and thanksgiving that flow from a business leader's heart full of this kind of faith change the countenance of the leader. This affects the way the leader interacts with his staff. In times of trial, this kind of leadership changes an organization, helping to put the organization in the best position for effectiveness through the trial.

9. Get in the "Zone." David uses a rich combination of metaphors in his psalms that we discussed as the "Zone" from which he led his business: under the shadow of God's wings, on a rock, in a fortress, in a refuge, in a tower, and behind a shield. This Zone is the place where our souls are secure, stable, and protected. David gives us great faith pictures that combine to define a Zone of strength and security as we lead. When you find yourself in times of trial, make sure you're in this Zone.

10. Expect deep blessing. David openly exposes the workings of his heart in Psalm 43 as he asks himself in verse 5, "Why are you in despair, O my soul? And why are you disturbed within me?" This great leader had the widely recognized leadership quality of optimism even though within his heart he actually felt the weight of trials and setbacks. He felt despair. He was disturbed inside his deeper thinking.

Man, have I ever felt that, and I bet you have too. One of the things that made David a great leader, however, was when he recognized his feeling of despair, he went on to say, "Hope in God, for I shall again praise Him, the help of my countenance and my God" (Psalm 43:5). Notice he didn't say, "Self, get over it because God is going to get you out of this." He told himself to hope in God because as he truly hopes in God, he knows

God will transform his heart and honestly change the way he feels—even about his trial ("the help of my countenance and my God").

So we are encouraged by the heart after God's heart to stay honestly in touch with what we're feeling in times of trial. And not only that, but to expect God to transform real despair into real optimism, an optimism so real that our feelings are changed. This steady and enduring optimism is grounded in the character of the God who lives in the Christian leader and His faithfulness to direct your real heart to real hope.

A good trial in our business should generate in us the certain expectation of a deep spiritual blessing yet to come: a blessing in the depths of our hearts, where we really live. This is exciting! And this transforms our business leadership in difficult times, at the core of our hearts.

Picture This in Business Trials

The guidelines above point to the value of trials in your life, even those trials you may have initially created, as you walk with God through those trials. Enjoying God's faithfulness while you allow Him to "make His love marvelous in your besieged city" is one more aspect of the heart after God's heart's character, and as this heart leads in building your business, it becomes another aspect to *Business after God's Heart*.

You might want to write these "Ten Guidelines" on an index card and tape it in your work area because we should expect trials every day. A handy reminder provides help when you need it and having the list where you can see it will help you expect trials. Or use your smartphone to take a picture of the table below and keep it in your Notes app for quick reference.

Business after God's Heart
Ten Guidelines for Trials

1. Rejoice in the expected trial.
2. Examine your heart for sin.
3. Examine your business for sin.
4. Maintain a short bad/long good perspective.
5. Pray in faith.
6. Wait in faith.
7. Do not fret.
8. Awaken praise and thanksgiving.
9. Get in the Zone!
10. Expect deep blessing.

CHAPTER 7

Leading with Humility and Confidence

But the humble will inherit the land and
delight themselves in abundant prosperity.
—Psalm 37:11

My friend Will is an entrepreneur who owns a technology services business. His company was fundamentally built on his background and credibility as a very bright engineer trained at the US Air Force Academy and on his accomplishments in technology management as an officer in the air force. He knew technology's application to support military programs and he had mastered the complex government procurement system. Will confidently applied his strengths to build a thriving company with annual revenues of $50 million and profits of over $7 million. In 1999, Will pivoted his company away from its core strengths in government technology services and toward the booming telecom market. Then in 2001, the telecom bubble burst and what little progress he made was lost.

Will retained me to help him rebuild what was left of his now $20 million government technology services business. Over the year or so that I worked with Will to pivot his company back to its core strengths, he spoke of his self-confidence that moved him to take great risks, lose tens of millions of dollars, and almost lose his entire company. And believe me: I could relate. I too had a great plan that seemed to be working incredibly well—gaining greater confidence in my business decisions, building a company to become an internet giant in terms of traffic and shareholder value—and it came down around my ears.

Humility and Confidence

Confidence is an inspiring attribute of a good business leader. My friend Will had great confidence. So did I. It's very important. But how does confidence coexist with humility? Can humility only be built on catastrophic failure? How is a Christian business leader genuinely confident and genuinely humble?

In my experience in working with business leaders, humility and confidence are words that don't seem to go together. While confidence is often mentioned as an important attribute of a business leader, it's never associated with humility. The closest we usually get to associating the two words is speaking of being humbled following overconfidence. For most of us, whatever confidence we have in business is based on our business skills and training which have been proven by our previous successes.

Not so with our hero, King David. He was a highly confident and humble leader. We will see that he had great confidence because of God's attributes, including His love, sovereignty, and power. He had great confidence because of the extremely high view he knew God had of him. And He had great confidence because of his certainty in God's ultimate triumph. David was also a humble leader, and he expresses this combination of humility with confidence for the Christian business leader head-on in Psalm 37:11 as the Spirit inspires David to tell us that "the humble will inherit the land." Recognize that for David, the land represents the basis for the business. In the agrarian economy of the time, the land is the basis to establish a business in crops and/or livestock. So the humble will inherit the basis for business, and they will "delight themselves in abundant prosperity" (Psalm 37:11). Abundant prosperity. The business of the humble will not just prosper; it will abundantly prosper. The Holy Spirit here, in Psalm 37, gives us this promise. The promise is based on the power of God, not on you and your business. Do you believe the humble will have a basis for business and will enjoy abundant prosperity? David did. You should. Like David, your confidence is wrapped up in your humility! The reason for your confidence is faith in God's power, not your business smarts; in fact, we are not even talking about what's going on in the business. If you really believe in God's power to bless your business, then you have confidence in your business. This confidence is built on

God's power and promises, not on your ability or business circumstances. So not only is this confidence not contradictory to humility, but this confidence reinforces true humility.

True Humility from the Heart

We will spend a longer time discussing confidence, but let's begin with a brief look at David's example of true humility. Psalm 131 shows us this extraordinarily confident leader also had a genuine humility.

> O Lord, my heart is not proud, nor my eyes haughty; nor do I involve myself in great matters, or in things too difficult for me. Surely I have composed and quieted my soul; like a weaned child rests against his mother, my soul is like a weaned child within me. O Israel, hope in the LORD from this time forth and forever. (Psalm 131:1–3)

At the core of David's being, in his heart, at the beginning of his thoughts, he is not proud; he says, "O Lord, my heart is not proud, nor my eyes haughty." We know his heart is humble because the eyes express the heart in ways that are true. It's much more difficult to control the look in your eyes than to control what you say. It's no great feat for a Christian business leader to say things that sound humble. David is saying that his humility is from the heart, in his very soul, and as a result it can be seen in his eyes.

Here this great man of God goes on to tell us true humility also does not lead the business to overextend. David was an extremely capable man who was extraordinarily blessed and gifted by God, but he tells us here that his genuine humility does not take him beyond God's leading, His provision, and His equipping. Overextending in business beyond God's planned reach, or presumptuously going ahead of the Lord, leads to danger, as David said. "Nor do I involve myself in great matters, or in things too difficult for me." In my consulting business, Will's is not the only company I've helped where leadership has overextended or is considering strategies that will overextend. It can be a difficult thing to fight as usually the root problem is pride, and people who are driven by their ego are easily deceived into exercising flawed judgment. It's difficult to reason with people in this state of mind. I have found that in these situations leadership is often flush with recent success and self-confidence is running high, while the objective basis for the venture under consideration is low. Humble business leadership keeps the business in its "wheelhouse," operating within its core strengths and not extending into areas where it is not qualified or areas where substantially more than the available resources are required to succeed. And because this humble leadership rests its confidence in God, God gets the glory as He prospers the business. The heart of David tells us that pride and the irrationality it breeds should be guarded against.

David's Confidence Was in God's Attributes

Pride and self-confidence are so bred into our business leadership culture it's difficult for Christian business leaders to identify it in their own hearts, much less root it out. This is especially true for folks who have already achieved significantly, consistent with the methods and expectations of the business world. Yet self-confidence, in the very best case, is a limited confidence, based on a false foundation, and it is ultimately a form of idolatry. Confidence, or faith, in all God is to the business leader is confidence that will not be shaken, regardless of the business circumstances; and it is a confidence that has no limitations.

David succinctly summarizes many of God's attributes in Psalm 103 as he opens up his heart to help us understand the source of his depth of confidence that was foundational to his greatness. So let's apply this psalm to your business life as we pray that the Lord would minister it to your soul, and use it to build your confidence in all that He is to you and your business—*with humility.*

God's Record Is Our Confidence

"Bless the LORD, O my soul, and forget none of His benefits," says David in Psalm 103:2. In the ebb and flow of day-to-day business, it's so easy to forget His benefits. Here we're encouraged to forget none of His benefits, only a few of which are outlined in this psalm. Here David encourages us to remember all of them. Usually, we get focused on all we must do and forget the benefits of being a child of the King of kings and Lord of lords. When we focus on all He is and all He has done for us personally, confidence in our present business circumstance comes very easily. This confidence is a confidence in God Himself.

God's Power to Heal Business Gives Confidence

God is the One "who pardons all your iniquities, who heals all your diseases" (Psalm 103:3). Remember that the God of the universe pardons all your sins. As a result, you can know you have been made pure and holy and, in fact, are in the presence of God almighty as you engage in the business of the day. All this is because of Christ's work on the cross; it's not based on anything that you have done. Once again, our confidence is in Him, and it reinforces genuine humility. This great and merciful God is also the one who heals you. If God can heal you from diseases, cuts, and bruises without your conscious effort, He can surely engage to do a mighty work in your business. Business "diseases" can shake your confidence, but you can be confident that the Healer of your body is just as much the Healer of your business. From this place you can, with David, draw confidence in Him.

God's Mercy and Power Give Business Confidence

"Who redeems your life from the pit, who crowns you with lovingkindness and compassion" (Psalm 103:4). Redeeming your life from hell represents some major lifting and is indicative of both God's power and His mercy, consistent with His love and compassion, which are just as focused on you today in your business endeavors as they were at the moment you were saved. It's not like His mercy and power on your behalf have somehow changed with time since you were saved, or that they only apply to your life at home or at church. You need His mercy and power for business today, and both are there for you. Because in your business you will fall short in strength, ability, and righteousness, you need God's power and mercy every day. It's there for you every day. Remember this. Consider with the heart of David that *you are "crowned"* by God almighty with His "lovingkindness and compassion" today in your business. Depend on it. And allow your real faith that He has crowned you with love and compassion to lift up your head on this business day.

God's Best Is the Best Confidence

"Who satisfies your years with good things, so that your youth is renewed like the eagle" (Psalm 103:5). Do you believe in this business day that God has good things for you? Do you have faith that God's ideas of "good things" are the best things that can happen to you in this business day? If you do, then your heart will share David's confidence for today. In Romans 8:28, the Spirit tells us, "And we know that God causes all things to work together for good to those who love God, to those who are called according to His purpose." When you are certain that God is going to work every angle of your current business experience together for His good result, beyond any good that you could imagine, then your confidence in your current circumstance can't possibly be shaken. It feels good to know the God of the universe is working everything together for good on your behalf. So much so, it feels like your youth is renewed. You're refreshed as you're feelin' it in your heart. You're soaring with real confidence—confidence in God!

God's Amazing Grace Builds Confidence

"The LORD is compassionate and gracious, slow to anger and abounding in lovingkindness" (Psalm 103:8). Today in business, remember that the Lord's compassion and grace are focused on you. Amid whatever the problem may be, your Father is there with you, and He has a heart of compassion for you. He feels what you feel. He cares, and He is the almighty God of the universe! That's a good Guy to have feeling your pain in this moment. And when the God of the universe is giving you grace, you've got underserved gifts that can transform a business situation. During business problems, believe He has the power to give you undeserved gifts of favor, consistent with His real compassion on you, His dear child. His grace is amazing in business! I've experienced God's grace in business at a scale that challenged my imagination or any expectation. If you don't believe in God's amazing grace in business, then you don't really believe in His amazing grace in your life because most of your waking life is spent at work. God's grace should be expected at work! So before there is a problem, approach your day with confidence that the compassion and grace of the God of the universe is present with you. This confidence is transformative at the depth of your soul, and for David, this confidence affected everything he touched. God gives you that same amazing grace to undergird your confidence in the details of your business.

God's Huge Love Builds Huge Confidence

"For as high as the heavens are above the earth, so great is His lovingkindness toward those who fear Him" (Psalm 103:11). Here David tries to put a measurement on the love God has for you. The height of the heavens above the earth is the measure of the love your Father in heaven has for you in the midst of whatever is going on in your business. In trying to measure His love for you, we see with David that the heavens are way up there. Just thinking about the height, or distance, to the farthest star is even more mind-boggling than David could imagine, and the heavens are above this by another whole dimension. That's a lot of love He has for you. The measure of God's love for you can also be seen in Christ's work. In 1 John 4:9 the Spirit tells us, "By this the love of God was manifested in us, that God has sent His only begotten Son into the world so that we might live through Him." The love of God was manifested, or made measurable, by our infinite God becoming flesh and making an infinite sacrifice in order to provide the measure of His infinite love for you personally. This infinite love for you has not changed after Calvary and it has not changed since you first received it. It's just as enormous and just as personal in each moment you have in your business as it was when you first believed. Knowing that the "height" of His infinite love for you was completely proven on Calvary, you must have confidence in His loving engagement on your behalf in business today.

God's Guilt-Free Confidence

David confidently says, "As far as the east is from the west, so far has He removed our transgressions from us" (Psalm 103:12). If your sins are confessed, you should have no nagging sense of guilt to compromise your confidence as you do business. Guilt can be extremely debilitating in business, and the only way to effectively be free from guilt is to have faith in the effectiveness of Christ's blood to completely remove our sin from your soul and make you holy at the very depth of your consciousness and even beyond your consciousness. David said you should be certain that your sins have been separated from you by an infinite distance—the distance that the east is from the west. As a result, God has equipped you to operate your business with *zero guilt*. Nothing should be bothering your conscience as you do His business in His presence and for His glory. This is a very confident position the Lord, in His grace and mercy, gives to the Christian business leader.

God's Intimate Compassion Builds Confidence

You should have confidence in business because the God of the universe is your loving Father and He really understands you. You are His baby! You should feel as totally secure in His compassionate arms as David did when he said, "Just as a father has compassion on his children, so the LORD has compassion on those who fear Him. For He Himself knows our frame; He is mindful that we are but dust" (Psalm 103:13–14). God is not far off from your business situation and only concerned about "church stuff." He understands what's going on around you and He really cares. And as He engages compassionately in your business life, He doesn't think you are some kind of super spiritual person. He knows that you are *only dust*. He has no expectation of perfection. In fact, He expects the very frailty you feel personally, spiritually, and in business. And understanding all this frailty, He loves you infinitely and He's going to take care of your business, consistent with His perfect compassion. And remember your compassionate Daddy has a wealth of resources beyond comprehension.

God's Eternal Love Steadies Our Confidence

"But the lovingkindness of the LORD is from everlasting to everlasting on those who fear Him, and His righteousness to children's children" (Psalm 103:17). David was grounded in his faith that God's personal love is not only infinite, but it's also eternal. It's not going to change with time. Jesus Christ, eternal God in the flesh, demonstrated God's eternal love for you by making the eternal sacrifice of Himself to prove the eternal love of God for you. In business, we all face the unknowns and "unknowables" of the future. As you face these unknowns ahead, you can be entirely confident, just as David was, because you are certain the future will come to you consistent with the unchanging love of almighty God. The One who loves you so has sovereign power over time and eternity and certainly all future uncertainties in your business.

God's Infinite Power, Personally Engaged, Builds Real Confidence

"The Lᴏʀᴅ has established His throne in the heavens, and His sovereignty rules over all" (Psalm 103:19). *This* is power—real power. David recognized God's power over *everything!* His power wasn't just for David's time or in a realm that is somehow impractical. He has sovereign power over your business. It's a fact. And best of all, this sovereign God is also the One who loves you infinitely, is your intimate Father, and understands all your business circumstances with perfect compassion. As you step up to lead in business today, you should be extremely confident in this great and mighty God who is engaged personally on your behalf. This confidence in Him transforms your character as it did David's, and as your character is transformed, so is your performance as a business leader. And so is your business.

Confidence in Him with True Humility!

Notice that there is *nothing* of personal pride in any of this confidence, because it's *all* about God, His greatness, and His personal engagement on your behalf in business and every area of your life. And confidence in God is totally consistent with true humility.

God Made You Just a Little Lower than a Star-Maker

In Psalm 8, the Holy Spirit inspires David to communicate God's extremely high view of us, which must have contributed greatly to David's confidence as a leader.

> When I consider Your heavens, the work of Your fingers,
> the moon and the stars, which You have ordained; what
> is man that You take thought of him, and the son of

man that You care for him? Yet You have made him a
little lower than God, and You crown him with glory and
majesty! (Psalm 8:3–5)

Here David steps back and looks at God's awesome creation. As he
meditates on the creation, the Holy Spirit uses it as an object lesson to
help us all understand the way God views us. Let's go with the heart of
David in considering the Lord's object lesson in Psalm 8. First David looks
at the heavens, the moon, and the stars. If it's a clear evening, take a break
now and go look up at the moon and stars. Enjoy the beauty. Consider
the perfect placement of the moon, reflecting the awesome light of the
sun to illuminate the night. Consider the almighty God who made them.
Consider the distance that is beyond comprehension to the nearest star.
Then consider the distance to the farthest star. Now consider the size, the
power, and the energy of each of these myriad "suns." Now consider the
awesome power and wisdom of God to create all this, place it in exactly
the right position, and sustain it all. This great God of all creation has
placed you just a little lower than He is. You are really close to being a star-
maker! He made you this way. And anyone who is almost a star-maker is
one who is crowned with glory and majesty! So have confidence, glorious
and majestic "almost star-maker!" Be as certain as the heart of David that
God gave you the right stuff!

   God has a job for you that He has fully equipped you to do, having
made you to be just a little lower than the Creator of the universe. David
tells you about God's plan for you to participate in exercising dominion on
earth through your business, as he continues his meditation in Psalm 8:6–9.

> You make him to rule over the works of Your hands; You
> have put all things under his feet, all sheep and oxen, and
> also the beasts of the field, the birds of the heavens and
> the fish of the sea, whatever passes through the paths of
> the seas. O Lord, our Lord, how majestic is Your name
> in all the earth!

Here the Spirit inspires David to tell you that God made you to rule over
His creation. He made you a little lower in power and ability for creating

the heavens but fully able to rule the earth. Your dominion over the earth on God's behalf is to be exercised primarily through the business that you lead. You should have confidence God has equipped and enabled you to execute this plan. By the very definition of who God has made you to be ("a little lower than God"), have faith that He has given you what's required to exercise this dominion, consistent with His plan. It's all about Him: His design for you, His power working through you, and His plan for you. As you recognize, by faith, that you are doing God's will in exercising this dominion over His creation rather than doing your own thing, God gives you confidence in Him for the business He has for you to do.

David concludes this meditation on God's design for you to rule over His creation with praise that flows from his heart. "O Lord, our Lord, how majestic is Your name in all the earth" (Psalm 8:9). Your dominion over God's creation is a beautiful thing and should result in praise to God. Just as creation itself brings praise to God, your dominion over creation should bring praise to Him.

Like many of you, I have stood at the rim of the Grand Canyon. There is no picture that could possibly do justice to this amazing sight. This amazing work of God's hands must bring Him praise. Similarly, I've looked out the window of an airplane at the Manhattan skyline. This amazing work of God, through man as his dominion over the earth is exercised, must also bring God praise. Whether I look at the Grand Canyon or the Manhattan skyline, I praise God for what His hand has done or for what man has done through His enabling. Your work and my work, the outcome of our labors, should bring God praise. He made us to exercise this dominion and it's a beautiful thing. When our work is focused on ourselves and is done with the strength of the flesh, the outcome glorifies ourselves. When we become so immersed in the world's view of business that we completely lose track of God's view, then we just consider it all an outcome of man's efforts, which are divorced from the Creator. This perpetuates a view of a separation of business from God and will lead us to a false confidence in our flesh, or a lack of confidence as we lead our business. Our work may not be as spectacularly large a sight as the Manhattan skyline, just as God's work in creating a butterfly is not the same as His work in creating the Grand Canyon. Examine a butterfly closely, however, and you are amazed at the wonder of God's creation in an entirely different way than you are amazed when standing on the Grand Canyon's rim.

Once you recognize that your business is an extension of God's creative power and design, as David did, it's easier to realize that doing your business is actually doing God's business. And just as it's God's plan for you to participate in His design to reach the lost with the message of salvation, it's also His plan for you to participate in His design to rule His creation. In this sense, you can know you are on a mission from God as you do business, just as surely as a missionary knows he is on a mission from God to reach the lost.

David had this perspective on his business, and you need to see your work as a mission from God so that it affects your attitude as you approach each day. It not only gives you confidence, but it also motivates you to give your very best effort since you're serving God. The Holy Spirit reinforces David's perspective on this matter of work in Colossians 3.

> Slaves, in all things obey those who are your masters on earth, not with external service, as those who merely please men, but with sincerity of heart, fearing the Lord. Whatever you do, do your work heartily, as for the Lord rather than for men, knowing that from the Lord you will receive the reward of the inheritance. It is the Lord Christ whom you serve. (Colossians 3:22–24)

This instruction is not to business leaders but to slaves. However, if a slave is to see his work for his master as service to the Lord, how much more should a business leader consider his work as a service to the Lord. We serve the Lord, not the owners of the business and not ourselves. So whether you're the top banana or not, you serve God as the business engages to exercise dominion over creation, in whatever little corner of the creation it's engaged. Our focus for business is on nothing less than the Lord. This should motivate us to do our very best as we walk in devotion to God. And we have confidence the Lord will reward our efforts. ("From the Lord you will receive the reward of the inheritance"; Colossians 3:24.)

Effectively exercising dominion, or business success, is God's will. It's His design from the beginning. David understood this very clearly.

His confidence was derived from the extremely high view of himself as "a little lower than God" and from his certainty that God had directed and empowered him to rule over the work of His hands through business.

Confidence in God's Preparation

David knew the Lord had prepared him for the mission He gave him to perform. In Psalm 144:1, David says, "Blessed be the Lord, my rock, who trains my hands for war, and my fingers for battle." David recognizes God's preparation strategically (for war) and tactically (for battle). War and battle were important parts of the "business" God had given him to do. The basis for David's courage in meeting his most famous conflict with Goliath was David's confidence in God's preparation through his experience in defeating lions and bears.

> But David said to Saul, "Your servant was tending his father's sheep. When a lion or a bear came and took a lamb from the flock, I went out after him and attacked him, and rescued it from his mouth; and when he rose up against me, I seized him by his beard and struck him and killed him. Your servant has killed both the lion and the bear; and this uncircumcised Philistine will be like one of them, since he has taunted the armies of the living God." And David said, "The Lord who delivered me from the paw of the lion and from the paw of the bear, He will deliver me from the hand of this Philistine." And Saul said to David, "Go, and may the Lord be with you." (1 Samuel 17:34–37)

Even at this early stage in his life, David was very clear in his understanding of God's preparation for the task at hand. When David was in training to protect his father's sheep, and when he was defeating wild beasts, he wasn't thinking about how it was preparing him to defeat a giant. When the giant stood before him, however, and he was presented with God's mission, he understood God's preparation. Later, as king, he recognized in the psalms that God had prepared him to be effective in the strategies and tactics essential for success as a warrior-king, consistent with God's mission for him to lead in taking and securing the Promised Land.

As a business leader, today you can look back on your life and say that your education, training, and experience have prepared you for the business challenges that you face. You could say you chose the right business or technical school; you were deliberate in selecting the right postgraduate opportunities for specific training or further education, and you have pursued jobs that have been orchestrated to define your resume in ways that prepare you for the job at hand. Or like David, you can look back and see God's preparation. By faith, you can be certain God, the God you know from Psalm 103 to be your compassionate Father who loves you beyond all measure, is also the sovereign God who rules over all. This merciful and all-powerful God has worked the details of your life to prepare you for the mission He, in His sovereignty, has now given for you to perform in your business. During the time of your preparation, you might have even been in sin and rebellion, and you might not even have been a Christian, but God was preparing you for this moment in business. David failed in many ways we've already discussed, but it was his faith in God's grace and mercy in his life to pardon, redeem, and heal that made his heart a heart after God's heart. So have faith that despite it all or because of it all, God has prepared you for what He puts in front of you now. You couldn't have known at the time your current business is what God was preparing for, just as David couldn't have known. David did look back and know who had prepared him; this you must know as well. And if God has prepared you, then you are prepared indeed.

Being certain God has prepared you puts you in position to continually put confidence in Him as you go through your current challenge. The heart of David was certain that God had prepared him very specifically for being effective in his vocational calling. He didn't say that he prepared himself for battle and war, even though he did actually have to practice and train vigorously. By faith, he looked back and saw all of it from God's hand of preparation. If you don't see your preparation as God's preparation, you will perpetuate the orientation toward self-confidence with all the associated limitations. Likewise, as you face the future, you can also be certain He is now preparing you for what you will face in the future. As a result, there is no uneasiness about future events but instead a steady confidence. Even as He previously prepared you for today's challenges in ways you didn't see at the time, He is also preparing you now for the missions He has for you in the future.

Confidence in God's Ultimate Triumph

While we are called to exercise dominion over the earth, and this can be done in large measure through our business endeavors, the heart of David exhorts us to keep in mind the ultimate dominion will happen when Christ returns to rule. This faith is what David writes about in Psalm 110. David was called to win battles and wars, conquer territory and exercise dominion, and while he does this, he sees through the eyes of faith God and His Son exercising a dominion yet to happen. This psalm provides a valuable eternal perspective for you on today's challenges in business.

> The LORD says to my Lord:
> "Sit at My right hand
> Until I make Your enemies a footstool for Your feet."
> The LORD will stretch forth Your strong scepter from
> Zion, saying,
> "Rule in the midst of Your enemies."
> Your people will volunteer freely in the day of Your power;
> In holy array, from the womb of the dawn,
> Your youth are to You as the dew.
> The LORD has sworn and will not change His mind,
> "You are a priest forever
> According to the order of Melchizedek."
> The Lord is at Your right hand;
> He will shatter kings in the day of His wrath.
> He will judge among the nations,
> He will fill them with corpses,
> He will shatter the chief men over a broad country.
> He will drink from the brook by the wayside;
> Therefore He will lift up His head. (Psalm 110:1–7)

The world and the challenges of business may seem great. However, when you gain God's perspective and see the enemies of Christ, your loving Savior, being made "a footstool for [His] feet" (verse 1), you should have comfort and confidence to proceed with the righteous path even though things may look bad.

You can also share David's confidence that the One you follow is not going to change the game on you later. His principles are eternal and He will not be changing. "The LORD has sworn and will not change His mind" (verse 4). The markets may change, the economy may change, but God's principles will not change. He will never bless dishonesty in sales or creative accounting. He will always bless righteousness and judge evil. There will never be some "new thing" in business that will cause His principles to be dated. Without a doubt, your long-range confidence in God's ultimate triumph forms a foundation in your soul that will impact your short-range business thinking.

Humility and Confidence Work Hand in Hand

David's tremendous reliance on the God of the universe, who made him just a little lower than God, gives him confidence for what God has for him to do. And we see this confidence is balanced by David's humble and rational view of his relevant gifts, abilities, and resources—all things the Lord uses to guide him to the exact work where he is to confidently apply himself. The heart after God's heart in business has confidence in God for His enabling strength and power to impact within the core strengths of the business. Guiding the business to this area of God-enabled effectiveness brings peace and comfort to the business leader and the business. So much so that David poetically expressed in Psalm 131:2, "Surely I have composed and quieted my soul; Like a weaned child rests against his mother, My soul is like a weaned child within me." What a beautiful picture. In this picture, there is nothing of the stress we have come to accept as part of the business way of life. Place yourself in this picture with David as you rest your confidence in your Father, the God of the universe, and with all humility, guide your business to effectiveness, based on God's enabling and consistent with your core strengths.

The heart of David guides us to deep feelings of humility and confidence that are mutually reinforcing, rather than contradictory, and are blessed by God in business. Real faith (faith as good as sight) in God's attributes as we observed from Psalm 103 forms a bedrock for the soul, upon which personal confidence is based as you engage in business.

Combining humility with confidence *in God* yields honest assurance, but not cockiness. It gives the business leader the ability to identify with and engage with employees, while still leading them to achievement as the Lord leads. Since humble confidence is God's design, it really looks good on a person. It was one of the great qualities of David's life, making him a superb leader, and is an important characteristic of the heart after God's heart.

CHAPTER 8

Real Team Building

Behold, how good and pleasant it is
for brothers to dwell together in unity.
—Psalm 133:1

My brand-new company sent my wife, Linda, and me to Maui for a team-building getaway. What a deal! I was president of a company that had just been acquired by a large publicly held firm. All the key people in the public corporation were gathering for a huge event that had been planned for some time. My wife and I were added to the attendee list after all the planning had been done, and I had no role to play. So along with sitting in on the activities planned for more than three hundred key individuals from my new company, I just had the very special (all-expenses paid!) treat to fly to Maui with my wife for an amazing work vacation.

What a great opportunity to learn my new company's culture. After we settled in on our flight, Linda and I talked about how my new company sure knew how to pamper its key people. As the new president of one of their divisions, I thought, *I'm going to learn a lot about how the "big boys" do team building.*

We arrived at the Maui airport and were greeted by company employees. They knew who we were, took care of our bags and transportation to the best resort on the island, and saw to every detail of our arrival until we walked into our luxurious room. We were elated as we stepped out on our balcony overlooking a perfectly manicured resort and the azure Pacific! We totally enjoyed the rest of that day together as others arrived and I anticipated the beginning of activities at dinner that evening.

Mayhem ensued. It became apparent over the next three days that this team-building event was unabashedly focused on manipulating clients and staff members to maximize each key managers' compensation. They weren't interested in doing marginally better, mind you, but making a *lot* of money—getting rich. In the end, this very expensive pep rally wasn't even really about the company at all, or about its objectives and working together to accomplish those objectives. It was a crass and raucous affair highlighted by displays of public drunkenness. The entire event culminated in an island-themed megaparty featuring the CEO being physically carried into the assembly on a decorated throne by eight big Hawaiian guys dressed only in thongs with leis. Linda and I watched from quite a distance as the crowd went wild. I took the entire experience as a direct signal that I should consider career alternatives.

Clearly, most attempts at corporate team building are not nearly as "exciting." Corporate retreats and social gatherings are perhaps more commonplace. Companies design these activities to build up the team based on the importance of elevating the enterprise above the individual. We want everyone to act in the best interest of the enterprise rather than self. Given the nature of humankind, this is a very tricky endeavor. The end of most team-building attempts amounts to little more than clever manipulations through persuasion and incentives. The cast of would-be executives on the old *The Apprentice* reality show provide a concentrated dose of the kind of team building we usually see in business. It boils down to who can manipulate others better to produce the best results in a grand effort of self-promotion. You can barely detect the selfishness in those who are good at it, and these are the winners. As a very old comedian once said, "Sincerity is everything. If you can fake that, you've got it made."

Leading to Real Unity with David

Honestly, I must tell you that so many of my attempts at team building went down this same road. When I paused to really understand my heart attitude, I came to see that I was just cleverer at disguising my manipulation of staff members than were my new friends I met on our Hawaiian retreat.

In Psalm 133, David gets to the heart of team building as he expresses the excellence of unity, since unity can be defined as a group behaving together in the best interests of one another for the accomplishment of a higher purpose.

> Behold, how good and how pleasant it is
> For brothers to dwell together in unity!
> It is like the precious oil upon the head,
> Coming down upon the beard,
> Even Aaron's beard,
> Coming down upon the edge of his robes.
> It is like the dew of Hermon
> Coming down upon the mountains of Zion;
> For there the LORD commanded the blessing—life forever.
> (Psalm 133)

This unity contains a depth that can't be created through persuasion, manipulation, or incentives. It is grounded in a depth of character created by God Himself. When the people of a business enterprise possess this unity, it is good, pleasant, and precious and will be blessed by God. So let's examine how it is possible to have this kind of team building—the kind of team building that God blesses—the kind of team building to which the heart after God's heart leads us.

Your Unity with God: That "One Thing"

The starting point for the real unity David described in Psalm 133 is your unity with God. We were designed by God to be united with Him in the Garden of Eden, and He sent His Son to redeem us so unity with Him could be our day-to-day experience. The "One Thing" that David sought was to dwell in the presence of the Lord (Psalm 27) and Jesus's prayerful desire was "That they may all be one; even as You, Father, are in Me and I in You, that they also may be in Us" (John 17:21). From here the power of God works in the life of the business leader and those he touches. This is the bedrock of character upon which the power of real unity in business can be built. Jesus extends this theme in John 15 as He taught us to abide, or live each moment, united with Him. "I am the vine, you are the branches; he who abides in Me and I in him, he bears much fruit" (John 15:5).

The business leader who skips over the need to personally "abide" in Christ as Jesus exhorts, or "dwell in His presence" as the heart of David sought, and heads off to build unity in business will not see God's power in these efforts for "apart from Me you can do nothing" (John 15:5). Instead of real power, this leader gets involved in all those manipulative conspiracies to imitate God's power seen in real unity. The beginning of leading business to the divine sweetness of real unity that David describes in Psalm 133 is found as we seek to dwell in God's presence as David did and there experience God's amazing love, as Jesus goes on to say in John 15:9. "Just as the Father has loved Me, I have also loved you; abide in My love."

When Love Is the "Tone at the Top," Real Unity Flows

"Tone at the top" is a phrase that is broadly accepted in referring to management's overall culture, normally alluding to ethical culture. Management's tone is said to have a trickle-down effect on employees as they tend to follow the examples of their bosses. If Christian business leaders are abiding (living) in *God's love*, we are living and breathing our business day in the midst of a whole lot of amazing love: perfect, unconditional love—eternal, infinite love. God's love! Living consciously in that kind of abundance of perfect love should make us a fountain of love. When a Christian business leader's "tone at the top" is a tone of God's unconditional love, it impacts everyone in every way within the leader's span of influence. And this positively builds unity. In fact, the Spirit in Colossians 3:14 exhorts us, "Put on love, which is the perfect bond of unity." The Spirit through David in Psalm 133 tells us that real unity that flows from this kind of love is precious and fragrant, it's noticeably transformative, and it's even holy. We'll spend the rest of this chapter taking a practical look at how the business leader's spiritual fruit of love can establish a godly tone at the top and practically impact team building and unity in the business.

Our guide will be the definition of God's love as it is famously expressed in 1 Corinthians 13:4–7.

> Love is patient, love is kind and is not jealous; love does not brag and is not arrogant, does not act unbecomingly; it does not seek its own, is not provoked, does not take into account a wrong suffered, does not rejoice in unrighteousness, but rejoices with the truth; bears all things, believes all things, hopes all things, endures all things.

Let's meditate together on this love and specifically apply these riches to business leadership and team building. As we put faith in the certainty that through Christ's work we are dwelling in God's presence (like the one thing that David sought), and that we are each moment completely immersed in His amazing love, we will overflow with this love for others in our business. This takes us to the details of the leader's heart, and it takes us to a depth of real love where the power of God is accessed to impact our relationships with our team and among team members. This is the kind of power that the heart of King David touched and it's the kind of power that transforms a leader's life and business. If we model this kind of love with sincerity, then we have taken the initiative to lead the organization to real unity and team building that many seek to counterfeit.

Patience and Kindness for Business Unity

The Christian business leader whose heart is like David's and who dwells in God's presence is patient. God's "love is patient" and the leader's patience is evidence of the leader's love for his staff on the job. You don't "try to be patient." You don't control your reactions when you're impatient with a failing subordinate. You are genuinely patient because you have faith you are, in that moment, united with the God of the universe who loves you infinitely. You also know God loves this subordinate the exact same way, even if the subordinate is unaware of God's love. So whatever the challenge stimulating the need for patience in the work relationships, the Spirit's fruit of patience is already there. There is no need to pretend or try to achieve it. When stimulated, if patience does not show itself in your business life, you know you have fallen into sin and lost focus of faith in your love relationship in the presence of the Father. Having detected sin, you quickly seek forgiveness and are restored again to yield to the Spirit as He produces this patience by His grace and for God's glory.

Kindness is a quality that is seldom associated with business leadership success. In fact, kindness can be perceived as a weakness for a results-oriented achiever. Yet the heart of the leader after God's heart is genuinely kind because "love is kind." Kindness is both a fruit of the Spirit and the definition of the spiritual fruit of love. Therefore, to the extent that kindness is not part of your package as a leader, we can say you are not united with God as you exercise leadership. Instead, you should be courteous and gentle, not because you must try to be that way but because as you dwell in God's presence, the fruit of your life includes these qualities. Your eyes look for opportunities to be helpful and your subordinates see the sincerity of your kindness directed at them. You serve as an example for the way things are done in your domain. Unkind actions begin to stand out as irregular and the tone of business is just different under your leadership. This leads to a type of team building that the business schools can only try to counterfeit. When you detect that kindness is not there in your business life, you know you must seek forgiveness, be purified by the power of Christ's blood, and engage confidently again as you, with David, dwell "in the house of the Lord."

Jealousy, Bragging, and Arrogance Destroy Unity

Jealousy is an ugliness that can pervade the business environment. The clever disguise it well or subtly use it to motivate greater intensity. Most recognize that jealousy is a negative motivator and the good team builders seek to manage away from it. The business leader with a heart after God's heart just simply is not jealous because "love is not jealous." You don't try to manage away from jealousy. You're just not jealous because jealousy is not love, and you genuinely love as a fruit of dwelling in God's presence. This means you genuinely rejoice with other's successes because, at your core, your love for them causes you to always hope for their best. As good things happen to others, rejoicing flows naturally rather than jealousy. As you genuinely delight in other's welfare, your countenance positively flows in your eyes, your facial expressions, and your actions. People see it and feel it. Another's achievement that benefits the business is really affirmed and all are made to feel more secure as they also seek to achieve, certain that they will be genuinely supported. As a result, they can focus their energies and their emotions productively to achieve for the enterprise. You set the example as you react and over time, others follow with a sincere depth of team building.

Bragging kills team building. It goes without saying that the heart after God's heart does not brag because "love does not brag." Bragging is ugly on anyone. In fact, the only one not repulsed by bragging is the braggart. Leaders are so often guilty of bragging because subordinates feel they must endure it to get along. Love, however, does not brag. Love would not seek to raise oneself up relative to those who are the objects of sincere and selfless love. When bragging begins, unity and team building subside. Bragging verbalizes self-absorption and there is nothing about self-absorption that unites and builds the team. When the leader is a braggart, there is no real team because everyone knows exactly the name of the game for this business operation. And the game is ugly and low performing.

An arrogant business leader does not unite the team for the same reason a braggart does not unite the team. Arrogance is all the attitude of bragging, without the words, and unlike bragging, it is a socially accepted hallmark of very many business leaders. "Love is not arrogant" because underlying arrogance is a sense of superiority. It is not so much a conscious attitude as it is a sincere, subconscious bias core to the way the leader interprets business and life in the transactions of every day. If you lead with a heart after God's heart, you are just not arrogant because you are broken, dependent, and humble. Your confidence is not self-confidence but a confidence in God. Your certainty of God's love for you extends to a certainty of God's love for others, even those who reject His love. At the core, you understand that in and of yourself you have done nothing to receive any blessing bestowed by God. You also understand those you work with are loved by God without any merit of their own as well. You are no better than anyone else you work with, and you have achieved nothing better in your own strength than the very least of them all. Those around you pick up on this genuine attitude that bleeds through in the subtleties, and they notice this is different from other bosses in the past. They sense you can be trusted for their best as they give their best to the enterprise.

Rudeness and Selfishness Undermine Unity

Because "love does not act unbecomingly," the business leader after God's heart would not do or say things that are rude or disrespectful—even though you might be able to behave in this way with impunity because of your position. Again, this is not something you have to try to avoid doing. As you live united with Christ, the Spirit has your heart in such a state of genuine love that rudeness or disrespect won't happen. Even in jest, the heart after God's heart does not speak or act in a way dishonors subordinates, even if such behavior is socially acceptable. As you are genuinely motivated by love and behave in this way over time, you build real trust of subordinates, and they know they are all pulling together for the best of the business.

A business leader who is not seeking self honestly wants the best for others before wanting the best for self because "love does not seek its own." Real love that flows from a heart united with God's heart has others first at decision time on the job. In love, it really does please the heart after God's heart to put others before self when considering office space decisions, making judgments that really could cost you, and selfless decisions nobody may know about. It doesn't take this kind of love to hold the elevator for someone, but it does to seek the best of others when dividing a limited bonus pool. This kind of love, manifested in real decisions that cost you and benefit subordinates, builds a real team as it transforms attitudes, builds trust and loyalty, forebears weaknesses and mistakes, and honors God.

Love Overcomes a Bitter Business Culture

Friction happens in business as folks of diverse backgrounds, worldviews, education, gifts, and abilities seek to work together to meet the objectives necessary for success. In this kind of environment, it is important to remember that "love is not provoked." God's Word does not say that love controls its reaction when it is provoked. It says "love is not provoked."

The real love God places in our hearts as we follow David's example to dwell in God's presence puts us in a place where even the best efforts of our associates to provoke us do not provoke us. We love them unconditionally and our love is therefore not dependent on their behavior. We understand that God made them completely differently and that He loves them infinitely, sending His Son to die for them too. However, when we are inevitably provoked, before we try to control our reaction and seek to fake it, we confess our sin, get forgiven and cleansed, and ask for God's love to fill our hearts to love them the same way He is loving them at that moment. The heart after God's heart leads away from provocation and away from the associated friction and conflict. When the boss leads like this, many will follow, and over time the culture of the business is transformed; fewer people are at odds, and all feel more united.

The business leader will be wronged at work. Count on it. Also, count on not receiving an apology. If, like David, you are "dwelling in the house of the Lord," united with Him as you were created to live, also count on His unconditional love in your heart for the one who wronged you, so you "do not consider a wrong suffered." In our culture today, it is very unusual for a person to acknowledge when they've wronged another and apologize, much less seek forgiveness. Folks have been trained from childhood to rationalize their behavior and muddle right from wrong to the point where there is almost never a need to set things straight. As a leader after the heart of God, our love for others in the workplace is such that wrongs suffered are not even registered as offenses on our part, so there is no need for an apology or any need for others to set things straight.

It is certainly better for the offender to apologize and seek forgiveness, but our love for the offender is not affected by the offender's action or inaction—apology or no apology. If we hold on to offenses, we've stopped loving, and while there may not be immediate evidence that we have sinned in not loving, there eventually will be. We will become bitter in time, and we will react later, slander sooner, or maintain a slow burn that will affect our judgment as well as our countenance. If the boss is bitter, it's easy for everyone to get bitter. "See to it that no one comes short of the grace of God; that no root of bitterness springing up causes trouble, and by it many be defiled" (Hebrews 12:15). On the other hand, if out of love we "don't take into account a wrong suffered," we stop the spread of sin that can defile many in the workplace. A bitter workplace is a place where people are critical, cynical, and backbiting, and it's a lousy place to work. The boss is the key to making sure it doesn't happen, as he lovingly "does not take into account a wrong suffered."

Loving Leadership Rejoices in the Things That Unite

In the workplace when you find yourself secretly (or perhaps not so secretly) delighting when there is moral failure, you are not loving as God loves you and you have fallen into sin because "love does not rejoice in unrighteousness." As a Christian in business, we are sometimes standing alone morally at work, and we are sometimes persecuted in subtle ways because of our righteous moral stand. As this happens, our hearts are still to love those who make us stand alone or persecute us. Jesus said, "Forgive them, for they know not what they do." And that it is to be our attitude toward those who isolate or criticize us for our morality on the job. If we find ourselves delighting in the moral failures of others at work, it shows us where our heart is, and it shows us we need to seek forgiveness from God. The leader who maintains a strong Christian testimony is one who is not only morally right but also loves the unlovely from the heart, as God loves them—even those that are morally wrong. Part of your strong testimony is your even-handed love for the moral and the immoral. This kind of love brings even those difficult ones together into a culture of unity set by the righteous leader and prayerfully compels them to grace and mercy in their time of need.

As a leader with a heart after the heart of God, you can have fun celebrating honesty because "love rejoices with the truth." The easiest thing in the world for folks to do at work is to lie when they *can't be caught* or shade the truth when they *can be caught*. As this happens, it propels a culture of distrust, inefficiency, and ineffectiveness. It costs money and creates frustration. It happens because such is the heart of humanity, but it also happens because there is perceived benefit from dishonesty and less perceived benefit from honesty. Others are fully aware when the truth is shaded, and they realize when benefits accrue to the person doing the shading. And so it spreads; a resulting distrust spreads, as does the loss of effectiveness of the organization. However, you can change this by focusing on the importance of real honesty when nobody's looking and rewarding such honesty as it's exhibited (and certainly not penalizing folks for their honesty). If honesty really does make you so happy you celebrate, even if this honesty exposes problems, then you will be leading the organization to greater trust and greater performance. All of this is part of excellent team building.

The High Road Takes You to Team Building

The leader after God's heart has the broad shoulders to bear up and love even when the temptation of succumbing to the world's way of seeing negative events, difficult coworkers, and challenging circumstances accumulates in volume over the long haul. "Love bears *all* things," not just the garden-variety, everyday things. When we think about loving others in business, sometimes we hope we'll get a return for our selfless acts of love from the person at some point. Or perhaps we think our love is an investment in future temporal business success. As soon as our expectation goes there, we've stopped loving these folks as God loves us (and them). God does not base the love He is giving us right now on our ultimate reaction, the scope of our sin, or only for some period. God bears with us in love through anything and everything. As you are united with Christ and love the same way He loves, your subordinates know the honest strength and depth of your care and kindness toward them. This security at their core builds the team and strengthens them to be candid regarding the real issues of the business and their personal difficulties so those business issues can be effectively addressed, and there can be windows of openness to minister to their personal difficulties.

God's team-building leader consistently takes the high road. Taking the high road is really what the Spirit means when He says that "love believes all things." A leader who "believes all things" assumes the best when interpreting statements or actions of others in the workplace. This business leader is not suspicious and does not waste energy wondering what kind of bad things people are up to. Suspicion can cloud judgment and irrationally affect the way you engage people. Assuming the best, on the other hand, maintains a positive, productive view of associates and it will bleed through in attitudes of trust and appreciation. This is not because you concentrate to always assume the best of others but because God's love really does fill your heart for the person who has said or done something that's subject to interpretation or suspicion. So it's not about managing reactions to events but about a depth of character rooted in God's love you are actually experiencing as you dwell in His presence, such that you are known for taking the high road in interpreting events. This depth of character supports your high opinion of associates, enhancing their job satisfaction, and it very substantially protects the organization from damaging employee relations and trust when good deeds are misjudged. While this depth of character may well result in some misplaced judgments, in the long run the overall impact will be to very positively build the team and shape the organization's culture of trust.

Envisioning the High-Performance Team

The love in the heart after God's heart honestly hopes for the best in the future for others in the workplace because "love hopes all things." There is an honest anticipation of better things, better attitudes, better actions, better performance, and better results. Love drives this leader to envision and expect harmony and teamwork, and your vision and expectation are so real you behave consistent with that expectation, having not yet seen such improvements. Your sincere heart that "hopes all things" pulls the character and culture of the organization forward into a better future of relationships and performance rather than merely letting what they've done so far shape your opinion. In this way, your heart after God's heart really does lead the team in moving forward in character and performance.

Loving leadership in the workplace is a marathon, not a sprint. There are new and varied opportunities to love every morning, yet the love of the leader after God's heart is a love that "endures all things." This means the character of your love at work does not have an expiration date or a breaking point. This can only be because it's really God's love. Each morning and each moment, as you are filled with the love God has for you, you are ready to engage with others consistent with the way you are loved by God. There is nothing in your love that anticipates a time when you're finished loving. This enduring strength of loving character is recognized in the workplace over time, shaping the character of the team.

Only through God!

This is the standard of real love on the job that flows out of a living faith that we are dwelling in God's inexhaustible and unconditional love. None of us will live there all the time, just as we know that David's heart desire was to live in God's presence each day and he still faltered. However, a leader who seeks to maintain an intense and practical understanding of the way you are loved by God as you abide in His presence will, over time, exhibit this depth of character through the way you love in the workplace. And to the extent you falter and God's love is not there, you know Christ came to *forgive and purify* you through His blood. This purity is very near to restore and position you to lead at work with real spiritual power and personal depth, which God sacrificed so much to provide. Our efforts will not produce this kind of love. Only by God's grace and mercy can we share the unconditional love He has so lavishly poured into our own lives. This kind of love is compelling. This kind of love applied over the long haul can build a real team. And this kind of team building is what God is all about.

Unity Is the "Tone at the Very Top"

God Himself is all about unity. He is One Father, Son, and Holy Spirit, and He relates to the business leader as One, having created all humankind in "Our" image to exercise dominion, ruling the creation practically through the exercise of effective business. "Let Us make man in Our image, according to Our likeness; and let them rule" (Genesis 1:26).

The starting point for the real unity David described in Psalm 133 is unity with God, just as Jesus prayed in John 17:21. "That they may all be one; even as You, Father, are in Me and I in You, that they also may be in Us." From this position of holy strength, as a gift of God's grace, the business leader is called to walk with God in business. Because of your position of leadership that God has arranged, it's possible for non-Christians and Christians in business to see the power of God flowing through a life united with Christ, in God's presence, immersed in His amazing love. From this strength, the heart after God's heart is in position to "put on love, which is the perfect bond of unity," as this tone at the top is established consistent with the tone at the very top. This 1 Corinthians 13-type love works its way out very practically in the leader's day-to-day engagement to love others in business, building unity in a real team that God will bless. This is a beautiful thing, and the Spirit through David tells us that this is good, pleasant, fragrant, pleasing, and it will be blessed!

CHAPTER 9

The Business of Praise

Every day I will bless You, and I will
praise Your name forever and ever.
—Psalm 145:2

David's Example of Praise

David's most enduring legacy is his praise. Others wrote of David's accomplishments, but David himself wrote about the deep issues of his heart and his heartfelt praise to God—the Source of all his achievements and strength. Even though David was neither priest nor scribe, the weight of his writing was focused on praising God. David understood completely that his effectiveness in business came from God, and his heart was steadied by his daily praise of the Author of this effectiveness in the business.

David said, "Every day I will bless You, and I will praise Your name forever and ever" (Psalm 145:2). In the psalms we have a treasury of this consistent daily praise. David's praise is core to who he is as a person. It not only expresses his heart but also shapes his heart, reinforcing his dependence on God and his confidence in God's enabling for the work He calls David to do. This establishes strength and stability, setting David up to be effective in all the various details and challenges of the business flowing to him daily as he does God's work.

What Keeps Leaders from the Business of Praise?

When I was a plebe and a new Christian at the Naval Academy, I attended an Officer's Christian Fellowship (OCF) talk during Plebe Summer. For context, Plebe Summer is the Midshipman's first summer at the Naval Academy, before freshman classes start. It is sort of akin to boot camp in that there is intense military indoctrination and tremendous pressure, causing many to wash out during the summer. The OCF speaker very powerfully challenged us to personal devotion and worship. After the talk, I approached the speaker to seek some solace because my life as a plebe was completely consumed with survival as I tried to keep up with demands designed to overwhelm me. I expected him to say something like "Hang in there, this time will pass soon enough, and you can get your life back to normal, including your time of praise and devotions." Instead, he looked me square in the eye and said, "If your God is important to you, then every day you will make time for devotion and praise." Then he turned and directed his attention to another.

This statement made such an impression on me that I can still, more than forty years later, remember everything about the room, the surroundings, and exactly what the speaker said. I remember the details because over the course of the last forty years—in crisis as an engineer at sea on a broken-down destroyer in the middle of the North Atlantic, in crisis as CEO of a publicly traded internet company, or later as CEO directing the turnaround of troubled companies—I have found Plebe Summer was certainly not the last time I would be overwhelmed. When I am overwhelmed, I remember the exhortation of that OCF speaker and my need to especially exercise the discipline of reserving extra time for devotion and praise.

Praising God is absolutely core to David's business. It's core to the heart after God's heart. Yet praising God is not part of the business leader lexicon. No book on building business will tell the business leader to make praising God an integral, daily part of the approach to business. This may be understandable for secular thought and writings. Even for a Christian business leader, however, the business of praising God is not very often a part of the daily routine. It's certainly not perceived to be an essential component of actually building the business.

Not so with David. We can perhaps think of many reasons we are not like David in our intensity to praise God. Fundamentally, the difference is we don't share David's faith in the vital presence of the God of the universe and the nearness of His sovereign power, personal enabling, and limitless unconditional love. If we have real faith in God's attributes, we must trust Him and not ourselves for our business, and like David, our faith and trust in Him will find expression in sincere praise in the context of our business.

Self-Confidence in Business Can Keep Us from Praise

The business leader who at the core is really trusting in self, rather than God, will find consistent praise does not come easily. The activity of praising God is by its nature not centered on the business leader who is offering praise. It's not about the leader's problems or opportunities and it's not about what keeps him up at night. Most leaders like to make progress with their activities, but the business of praise is endless so when we have finished for today there is still as much praise to offer tomorrow. It's not something that can be added to our list of accomplished tasks. In addition, praise is not focused on the leader's insights or his abilities, and in the end, it does not elevate the leader in any way. As a result, if we're really trusting in ourselves then praising God will seem hollow and of no practical value. If you're still on the throne of your business life, then praising God will feel hypocritical, like you are pretending He is on the throne. Praising won't come naturally; it will be awkward and contrived. As a result, it may become at best some kind of legalistic discipline like Jesus spoke of in Matthew 15:8. "This people honors Me with their lips, but their heart is far away from Me."

Sin Keeps Us from the Business of Praise

A heart that has sinned in business will not want to go through the charade of pretended trust in God for business. None of David's praises came from a sinful heart. Yet from our discussion in chapter 2 on "Doing Business with a Clean Heart," we know David to be far from perfect. He sinned *big time*. So we realize there were times when our great example of praise did not praise God. David spoke of a period when he was very far from praising God. "When I kept silent about my sin, my body wasted away through my groaning all day long. For day and night Your hand was heavy upon me; my vitality was drained away as with the fever heat of summer" (Psalm 32:3–4). During this time of sin and denial, David did not feel "in the mood" to praise God. In fact, he was under the heavy hand of God to help him see his need for repentance. And while he is our wonderful example of a heart after God's heart, an essential part of that heart is his humble recognition to need forgiveness and cleansing only God can provide.

We've already examined David's great prayer of confession and repentance in Psalm 51, but now we see that David sought this forgiveness so he could get back to this life of praise he cherished. He said, "Deliver me from bloodguiltiness, O God, the God of my salvation; then my tongue will joyfully sing of Your righteousness. O Lord, open my lips, that my mouth may declare Your praise" (Psalm 51:14–15).

Like David, there will be times when we sin, and in those times the imperative is confession and forgiveness so we can return to praise. When we do not feel in the mood to praise God, we should check our hearts for sin. A sinful heart will not want to praise God. A sinful heart will want to busy itself with just about anything but praise. The good news is forgiveness and restoration are as near to us as they were to David. When we sin, like David, we can say,

> I know my transgressions and my sin is ever before me. Against You, You only, I have sinned and done what is evil in Your sight, so that You are justified when You speak and blameless when You judge … Purify me with hyssop, and I shall be clean; wash me, and I shall be whiter than snow. (Psalm 51:3–4, 7)

From this position of being purified through the effectiveness of the blood of Christ, we're in position to say with David, "O Lord, open my lips, that my mouth may declare Your praise" (Psalm 51:15).

Beginning the Business of Praise

If we really believe in the reality of God's greatness and know for certain this great One is very near to us, engaging in our lives and present in our thoughts, then we can't help but respond with praise.

David's Willing Heart

Psalm 22 is a messianic psalm wherein David prophetically speaks the very words of Christ. David was inspired to give us His command to praise God in verse 23. "You who fear the Lord, praise Him; all you descendants of Jacob, glorify Him, and stand in awe of Him, all you descendants of Israel." And while David speaks this command of Christ, we just saw in Psalm 51 that he asks God to help him fulfill the command "O Lord, open my lips, That my mouth may declare Your praise." God clearly expects our praise, but we understand from the heart after God's heart that God is not far off, watching to see if we get it right. Instead, God is near to us, and He is there to help us as we ask Him to open our mouths and give us the words to praise Him, as He has commanded.

Like David, our obedience to the command to praise God simply begins with willingness. As busy business leaders, this willingness can be expressed by integrating the business of praise into our day as we put it on our calendars or our to-do list. With this willingness, we go to the Lord with a sincere and humble heart, and we ask Him to help us praise Him. We can be absolutely certain this prayer is consistent with God's will, and this is a prayer God will answer. So we have the command and the enabling, both from God. How encouraging it is for the business leader to know that when David, the great leader of Israel and the great author of so much praise, humbly went to God and asked for help to fulfill His command to praise Him, God delivered. And so He will do for each of us.

David's Faith in God's Greatness and Nearness

We look again at David's prayer in Psalm 8. Here David defines the fundamental basis to praise God is for His majesty and power. Yet David also articulates the nearness of God's engagement with the humble heart.

> O LORD, our Lord, how majestic is Your name in all the earth, who have displayed Your splendor above the heavens! From the mouth of infants and nursing babes You have established strength because of Your adversaries, to make the enemy and the revengeful cease. When I consider Your heavens, the work of Your fingers, the moon and the stars, which You have ordained; what is man that You take thought of him, and the son of man that You care for him? (Psalm 8:1–4)

The greatness of God is seen here in both His majesty above the heavens and the simple strength of a nursing babe. David is in awe and praises God when he considers His power to create the moon and stars yet to still focus His thoughts and care on people. He focused it on a person like David and on you while you engage in your business day. His greatness is not far off where we may admire Him with fear, but His greatness is very close and personal for you. This stimulates a heart response of praise as we in sincerity feel both His intimacy *and* His power. A business leader who is so moved by both God's intimacy and His power to then give praise to God is a leader who's stable to the core, strong but still humble, and extraordinarily confident. That's not the objective of real praise of God; it is an admirable by-product the world can only try to imitate. This is part of the character of King David that God offers to you and me.

In Psalm 29 we see David praised God for His awesome power and glory to have made it all ("ascribe to the LORD the glory due his name"; verse 2), to change things thought unchangeable ("the voice of the LORD breaks the cedars"; verse 5), and to continuously rule over it all, now and forever ("the LORD sits enthroned as king forever"; verse 10). A leader who is so personally and intimately connected with our great God that his emotions emit real praise from his heart is a leader with enormous depth of character.

David shifts to conclude this psalm by praising God for His engagement with people to give strength and the blessing of peace. "The LORD will give strength to His people; The LORD will bless His people with peace" (Psalm 29:11). So this One, with power beyond our imagination, is not far off, *and* He is giving strength to His people—to you and me. And He is the same One that is present in our thoughts, as we saw in Psalm 139:4. "Even before there is a word on my tongue, behold, O Lord, You know it all." And this One is right there in that thought and the next with tenderness, love, and protection. "You have enclosed me behind and before, and laid Your hand upon me" (Psalm 139:5). Understanding—really believing— the God of universe, with awesome power beyond all comprehension, is also intimately in my thoughts with tenderness and care is a totally mind-blowing truth that must cause me to praise Him! As David said, "Such knowledge is too wonderful for me; it is too high, I cannot attain to it" (Psalm 139:6). David's high and soaring view of God is so great that he must burst forth with praise. Imagine the psyche of a leader so filled with praise. Think about what it would be like to look into the eyes of such a leader. What excitement this leader would bring to a company! And think about how this extremely positive energy could transform those around this leader.

As we examined David's example of brokenness in chapter 3, we saw that David, more than any other person, understood the magnitude of Christ's sacrifice. The Spirit inspired him to speak Christ's very words and prophetically experience a part of Christ's sacrifice, as David says in Psalm 22.

> My God, my God, why have You forsaken Me? I am poured out like water, and all my bones are out of joint; my heart is like wax; it is melted within me. My strength is dried up like a potsherd, and my tongue cleaves to my jaws; and You lay me in the dust of death. For dogs have surrounded me; a band of evildoers has encompassed me; they pierced my hands and my feet. I can count all my bones. They look, they stare at me; they divide my garments among them, and for my clothing they cast lots. (Psalm 22:1, 14–18)

Our hearts fill with praise as we consider with David the magnitude of Christ's sacrifice: giving up the glory of heaven, submitting to human birth, dying a cruel death, and ultimately paying the penalty for the sins of humanity. This tremendous personal work of grace, mercy, forgiveness, and love Christ demonstrated on the cross was all aimed at our hearts and should bring forth our praise. David's soaring praises in Psalm 103, as we discussed in chapter 7, reflect his heart's exhilaration at the thought of God's majestic yet intensely personal work of forgiveness, redemption, and complete purification, along with His measureless personal love, mercy, compassion, and understanding.

As you begin thinking about the business you must do each day, you can have faith in your great God and His certain engagement in your thoughts with power, tenderness, and care, and you must respond with praise! Your praise is the consequence of who He is to *you*. It's totally about Him but directly personal for you. Now it can also be happening simultaneously with others (and that's an awesome and totally appropriate experience), but if it's not happening *personally* for you, you're only a witness rather than a vital participant in a divine event. Praise is the evidence you are enjoying His loving intimacy with you, in all His power. What an enormous position of strength for your heart. Doing business from this position of praise prepares your heart to interpret the business with the heart of God and do business after God's heart.

David Gave Praise an Appointment

For many of us, this idea of praising God in the business context is a new one. We really do trust Him with life and business, even participate in church services where God's praises are sung, but beyond this we have not considered the imperative King David felt to praise God in the context of his job. Now understanding the imperative and the blessing of giving praise as we work, we may be uncertain about how to get started. As we've discussed, an honest desire or willingness to respond to God's greatness with praise is the first and most important ingredient to our ability to praise.

We business leaders are a very busy lot. If we are not really living an honest faith in God's attributes and trusting Him with the business, then the schedule will fill in and praise will not get an appointment. While we want praise to come very naturally in the moment, being deliberate in substantiating our willingness to praise God will help make it happen as we develop new habits and thought processes for the workday. We all employ some method of prioritization to make sure we schedule in the essential appointments and focus our time on the things able to move our business forward. By the time we schedule all the activities we know will "move the needle" for the day, there is often no time left for praise. Praising God is not viewed as an item yielding a return on our labor (it's not going to "move the needle"), so it is pushed off the calendar—if it was ever on the calendar in the first place. I learned the same lesson during Plebe Summer: if I can't seem to find time to praise God, then I see fundamentally where my heart really is and what I'm really trusting in for my business. When our schedules do not allow time for praising God, we forfeit the opportunity of being a confident and steady hand at the helm. Instead, we will add to our busy-ness the anxiety, stress, and uneven temperament of ones dependent on our own devices rather than on the powerful and loving God of the universe.

If praise is a priority, it will be an important appointment you won't miss. What appointment is more important than your appointment to praise the God of the universe, who is personally engaged in every detail of your business and in the midst of your every thought as you engage yourself in the business? Praise was David's daily habit as he said, "Every day I will bless You, and I will praise Your name forever and ever" (Psalm 145:2). And as we've seen, consistent praise will shape your heart to be after God's heart as well.

Praising God with David

Now that we have put praise on our calendar, we can get right into it by opening the psalms and joining into David's praise. "O magnify the Lord with me, and let us exalt His name together" (Psalm 34:3). Amazingly, David invites us to participate with him in his praise of God. Since David filled the psalms with his praises, there is abundant opportunity to do just that. David is such a great example to us in so many ways, and here we can see him as our example and also as our "partner" as we participate with him in praising God. By the power of the Holy Spirit, we can transcend the ages and join in with this amazing leader who possessed a heart after God's heart in giving praise from our hearts. It may be helpful to picture David showing up to your praise appointment as you go to the psalms.

Remember David was a leader, much as you are, and although God used him mightily, he also was beset with human frailty, just as you are. As it turns out, David was a lot like you, so identifying with him as you share his praise should build your faith and expectation God will use your praise to shape your heart, as He did David's.

A Quick Guide

David's inspired praises are contained in almost all his psalms. Psalm 145, in addition to exhorting us to praise God every day, is a fairly comprehensive guide for praising our Lord. It might be good to open your Bible and enjoy praising God through this whole psalm. Here, we'll just walk through the first five verses together, thinking about the meaning of the praises and making them personal, as we participate with David, expanding on his inspired thoughts, and making them our own meditation of praise.

"I will extol You, my God, O King, and I will bless Your name forever and ever. Every day I will bless You, and I will praise Your name forever and ever" (Psalm 145:1–2). We see here we can speak directly to God, because God is "my God" just as He was "my God" to David. My God is right before me, or I before Him, and He is present in this moment with my praise. My God, You are personal and intimate with me. And You are "King," my King, ruler of my life, sovereign over the world, ruler of my business, and sovereign over the economy of man. I will bless Your name now, but I will also bless Your name forever in eternity. I'm certain, because of Your work to save me and make me holy in Your sight, I will praise You for Your work in doing this now, and for all eternity, regardless of whatever is going on in my business today. No matter what's on my calendar today, it is absolutely certain I will be praising You for all Your wonders for all eternity.

"Great is the LORD, and highly to be praised, and His greatness is unsearchable. One generation shall praise Your works to another, and shall declare Your mighty acts" (Psalm 145:3–4). You, Lord, are great! You are huge in power, love, mercy, and goodness. You are so great that I can't define Your greatness as it extends in every dimension of Your character beyond any measurement and beyond my ability to understand. I can only respond with the highest praise that I know how to give You. I will watch for Your mighty acts in my business today, I will tell my spouse and children of them tonight, and we will praise You together for Your greatness.

"On the glorious splendor of Your majesty and on Your wonderful works, I will meditate" (Psalm 145:5). We continue to think together with David about "the glorious splendor of Your majesty." There is so much to say about Your greatness that it's hard to find the words of praise suitable for You. I want my emotions to run with David's in thinking of Your greatness, not holding back the abundance of what might be said about You. For You are beautiful, glorious, splendiferous, powerful, majestic, awesome, and all these things multiplied, combined, and concentrated. And incredibly, amazingly, You deeply care about me and my business today. Praise Your name!

Continue yourself with this meditation through the psalm, dwelling with David on each phrase, allowing his inspired words to spark your own praise for your great God. David is not beyond you and his words are inspired to inspire your own. Be certain of God's intimacy in your thoughts as you give Him your willingness, knowing that He will help you with your praise. Through this one psalm, you will cover a very broad scope of praise, touring God's attributes as you spin off David's wonderful poetry covering His intimacy (v. 1), sovereignty (v. 1), eternal greatness (vv. 2, 3), wonderful works (v. 5), awesome acts (v. 6), abundant goodness (vv. 7, 9), righteousness (vv. 7, 17), grace (v. 8), mercy (vv. 8, 9), glory (vv. 11, 12), power (v. 11), majesty (v. 12), dominion (v. 13), care and sustenance (vv. 14, 20), provision (vv. 15–16), kindness (v. 17), presence (v. 18), answers to prayer (v. 18), salvation (v. 19), care (v. 20), and holiness (v. 21). This is just one psalm. The book of Psalms is a treasury of David's praise, and each verse can provide a meditation of praise sufficient to bless your soul and through you impact your business each day.

Document Your Praise

David sets a great example of documenting his praise. In fact, in the psalms we have are more than just a document of his praises, but we also have his praise communicated in the transparent context of his trials, his confusion, and his perplexities. The psalms are notes on David's heart, and his heart is full of praise to his great Father. The heart after God's heart kept a record of his heart's interaction with God. From this we are encouraged to keep a record of not just our praise but also our praise in the open and transparent context of our life.

I've kept notes of my prayers and praises for years. My habit was to get to work very early (beating the traffic) and conduct my devotions at my office desk, and for a long time, I documented my prayer and praise on note slips from my office desk. I kept those slips in a desk drawer, and over the course of time and office moves, I regretfully misplaced them. More recently, I began keeping one journal for business and for prayer, devotion, and praise. For me, this has been very helpful in integrating my praise with my business day, and I think it also brought me a little closer to the way David operated.

I've always kept a business journal wherein I take notes on meetings, conversations, business thoughts, and insights. Taking notes improves my comprehension and helps make me a more active and attentive listener. I can also look back to remember great things people have said, insights I might have had at the time, and I also use it as I prepare for decisions to refresh every meeting, conversation, and all my thoughts on a topic.

Now I have a single journal that I use for devotions and business. It includes all the notes I've always kept on business as well as my notes on my meditation in the Word, *and my praises from that day.* In the middle of a meeting discussing a business issue, as I take notes, I can look up at my praises from earlier, and even spontaneously add to those praises as they relate to current events. Not only does this maintain a record of praise but it also helps keep me centered on praise, making the praise of God part of my lifestyle, moment by moment. Further, as my praise and devotions are integrated into my daily planning, my heart is better prepared and even guided to better places. I've found that a single journal for praise, devotion, and business helps me maintain a single mind of dependence and reinforces my practical faith and reliance on God for each business moment.

Writing our praises down brings God's greatness and our adoration of Him into our physical world, and this is a particularly powerful aid to our mindset if it is done in the context of business. Things written down are concrete and we can physically see them. Whereas things that we only think and don't write down or speak out loud remain inside our minds. So maintaining a physical written record of those praises for His attributes and His active engagement in our business life brings Him more consciously into our physical world and reinforces the certainty of things previously only existing in our minds. And as we review our journal of all the notes and thoughts from meetings, we are also reviewing all our praises and insights from God's Word that may or may not be directly related to business decisions. But our business decision process is immersed in our active experience of the Spirit in various business days and is a reminder of God's hand shaping our hearts to praise Him on those days as He shapes our hearts to praise Him in the midst of the decision at hand.

The psalms are a great help to us in stimulating praise with David, and our own praises that we document can stimulate more praise as we review them and experience them afresh, much as we would a psalm of David. The same Spirit that inspired David is working in your heart and you are experiencing Him as David did. You're not just learning more about Him in the Word, you are knowing Him personally, and your praise brings vitality to that relationship just as it did for David. When all this is happening directly in the context of your business day, it is powerfully transformative to each of your days. And since we know that the majority of our life that we're awake is lived in business, we are actively praising Him in business or we don't praise Him very much.

David Makes It Vocal

We certainly can and should praise God silently in our hearts as we meditate on His greatness. Praise is totally appropriate and intended to be done silently. It's also intended to be done out loud. David said, "My mouth will speak the praise of the Lord" (Psalm 145:21) and "My tongue will joyfully sing of your righteousness" (Psalm 51:14). David is speaking and even singing God's praises. Notice he is using his mouth and his tongue! This is not just going on in his mind, but the great things he thinks about God are registering as words formed with his tongue, breathed from his lungs, and spoken out of his mouth so that his ears hear and the ears of others hear. David is very specific in speaking of his lips engaging in praise because we're to understand it's a physical event. He's making sound waves in his world, bringing praise to life!

He spoke of physically lifting up his hands in praise in Psalm 63:3–4. "Because Your lovingkindness is better than life, my lips will praise You. So I will bless You as long as I live; I will lift up my hands in Your name." These physical actions bring God's attributes and works out of David's mind, and they become physical sensations, sounds, and movements. If others only thought about God's work and only praised Him silently, He could be doing great things in their lives, but His great works would not be as evident to us. We are unable to praise Him equally with them. What He has done is more evident in our physical world as it is spoken, shouted, or sung. When we speak God's praise at work, it's noticed. While only some may participate with us or say the amen to our praise, God's glory is manifest right there. God has been brought into the business consideration, and there is no denying what He has done for the person speaking His praise. Spoken praise, delivered in humility at work, is still politically correct, even in the most godless environments. While it can become almost a cliché of false modesty among some, if God is genuinely thanked or praised from the heart among those who know you, they know that He is at work in your life. You have brought Him out of the unseen world where the unbeliever or nominal Christian would like to keep Him and put Him in their midst, not as a benign observer but as the sovereign God of life and this business. And when you speak praise to God in the workplace, you are changed—and so is the workplace.

Praise Changes the Business

Praise Builds a Crescendo of Faith

We can read about God's attributes and works and understand more about God as we study. Clearly, we see in the psalms that David was not just a student of God's attributes, but he also lived in the midst of all that God is, and living there, the Spirit generated praise as a fruit of David's real faith. David's faith moved from his mind to his heart and changed his feelings so strongly that praise happened. James famously talked about the right outcome of real faith, as he wrote,

> Even so faith, if it has no works, is dead, being by itself.
> But someone may well say, "You have faith and I have
> works; show me your faith without the works, and I will
> show you my faith by my works." You believe that God is
> one. You do well; the demons also believe, and shudder.
> But are you willing to recognize, you foolish fellow, that
> faith without works is useless? (James 2:17–20)

Faith in God and His attributes will produce your "work" of praise just
as it did in David's life. Real praise is the evidence of real faith. When we
engage in praising God, we go beyond knowing about God and intellectual
"belief" in His attributes. As we see from James, even the demons know
about God and His attributes. In fact, their knowledge of Him makes
them shudder. They do not, however, praise Him. When we praise God, it
shows we have real faith because only faith that is acted upon is validated
as real faith.

When we act on our faith by praising God, it builds our faith still
further. When we act on our faith, God affirms that faith in our hearts.
As we look again at God's definition of faith from Hebrews 11, we see that
"faith is the assurance of things hoped for, the conviction of things not
seen." We have faith in things that are unseen. Faith registers reality to our
mind at the same place that our senses (including sight) register reality to
our mind. Praise shows God's attributes are real to us in our minds—as
sure as if we could see, hear, and touch them. As we praise, the reality of
what we say about God becomes sound at that place in our minds where
our senses register reality, and it affirms that reality for us. Praise registers
faith to our senses, affirming and building the faith that already exists to
generate greater faith. When we speak, shout, or sing praises, and together
with others shout or sing about God's attributes, those attributes become
more real to us. Our faith is reinforced, generating still more praise, and it's
God's will that this crescendo of faith and praise build higher and higher,
individually and corporately, all for God's glory.

So whereas it is true our faith generates praise, it is also true our praise
confirms and builds our faith. And nothing so fundamentally changes
everything about the way a business leader engages to run his business as
what the leader honestly believes. Not what the leader thinks should be

believed or what the leader makes people think is believed but what the leader really believes will drive the way the leader operates. So the leader who daily praises the Lord, as David did, will be changed at the core, as David was, as this leader's praise builds even greater faith in God's power, sovereignty, omniscience, justice, mercy, love, forgiveness, and grace. This leader is leading from the Rock and says with David, "The LORD lives, and blessed be my rock; and exalted be the God of my salvation" (Psalm 18:46).

Real Praise Changes Your Heart

Responding to God's greatness with praise reflects a heart that really does have faith in His attributes and His works. When sincere praise happens, there has already been a work of faith in the heart. Your faith (as good as sight) in God's attributes makes those attributes such a certainty that it becomes core to who you are as a person. This goes beyond an intellectual understanding because the attributes and works of God are of such enormity and direct business relevance to you. This real certainty about who God is must transform the way you feel about your business. David said, "I will give thanks to the LORD with all my heart; I will tell of all Your wonders. I will be glad and exult in You; I will sing praise to Your name, O Most High" (Psalm 9:1–2). His response of praise was given with all his heart. David understands His great God. He does not admire from afar but engages himself deeply just as he has been engaged with by God. He engages emotionally because God's greatness has affected him emotionally. With his whole heart, he experiences the amazing blessings of God's character, made personal for him, and he is glad. David is a happy soul, and this happiness is an abiding and unshakable happiness because he exults in the God of the universe, not in some temporal success or personal recognition. In Psalm 33 David encourages our hearts to sing for joy in the Lord.

> Sing for joy in the LORD, O you righteous ones; praise is becoming to the upright. Give thanks to the LORD with the lyre; sing praises to Him with a harp of ten strings. Sing to Him a new song; play skillfully with a shout of joy. For the word of the LORD is upright, and all His work is done in faithfulness. He loves righteousness

and justice; the earth is full of the lovingkindness of the
LORD. (Psalm 33:1–5)

Sincere praise changes the leader's countenance. Here David says, "Praise is becoming to the upright" (Psalm 33:1). Praise looks good on a business leader. The business leader that fully engages his heart with praise looks better because the expression of praise flowing from faith in God's wondrous and personal attributes changes the leader's heart. Happiness can't be hidden. And when you personally experience God's greatness, His infinite and unconditional love, together with His limitless power, His victory over death, and His forgiveness, you should not contain your celebration! "Sing to Him a new song; play skillfully with a shout of joy" (Psalm 33:3). Your real faith in all He is and has done is so certain that you feel it. This is much bigger than winning a big contract or scoring a big bonus.

Right now, think of the biggest business success you could possibly achieve—a success so big it stretches your imagination or a success that secures a lush retirement. Got this pictured in your mind? If it just happened, what would this feel like? If that success suddenly happened, wouldn't you shout out loud? Well, better than your most aggressive imagined business success is what you have already received *right now* in Christ. Faith as good as sight in the unseen attributes of God and their relevance for your life is of such personal enormity that it changes your heart, and it generates a shout. "Shout joyfully to God, all the earth; sing the glory of His name; make His praise glorious" (Psalm 66:1).

Things are different for you in your business day and the difference is regardless of whether the business is trending up or down. You are centered, happy at the core, and prepared to walk with God through the temporal ups and downs of business each day. You're more optimistic, a better leader, and a better witness. Your heart, like David's, is after God's heart.

A Business Life of Praise

As a leader, warrior, and ruler, David had the challenges of a business leader, and he left us a record of his praise. Praise was a business discipline for him because he really understood the greatness of his God. In his God, David trusted, and through his God, David derived his strength, direction, and blessing in the business God had given him to do. For us, that means we must put praise on the calendar as an important appointment we can't miss.

While we're commanded to praise God, we also know from David that God will help us as we are sincerely willing. So ask God to help you praise Him, just as David prayed, "O Lord, open my lips, that my mouth may declare Your praise" (Psalm 51:15). And as He prompts you to praise Him, follow through with His praises as He does indeed "open your lips." And as you see God deliver at work, humbly and sincerely speak His praises from your heart to those around you. Your heart will be changed, your business environment will be changed, and you will function better for God's glory as you exercise dominion through your business for Him.

CHAPTER 10

David's Prayer for You

May the LORD answer you in the
day of trouble! May the name of the
God of Jacob set you securely on
high! May He send you help from the
sanctuary And support you from Zion!
—Psalm 20:1–2

I've experienced plenty of trials in business over the more than twenty years that I've studied the heart of David as I've led six very different companies across diverse trials. And the Spirit has ministered deeply to my heart as I've come back to the psalms of David with all my notes from years of meditation. After all these years of seeking to have business after God's heart from the application of David's psalms, I became CEO of a troubled company, and I was not quick to recognize that the troubles with the company were my spiritual trials—even after having drafted chapter 6 of this book on trials! A few months into the job, as I understood the magnitude of the "trouble," my heart felt the real weight of my "day of trouble"—my trial. As the CEO, I was responsible, and I had an overwhelming fear of failure. At this late stage in my career, it appeared as though my last gig would be a magnificent disaster.

The weight of all these thoughts and feelings yielded anxiety, stress, and sleeplessness. Alarm bells started going off in my consciousness about the condition of my heart. In my despair, I went back again to David's psalms, my notes, and sections of this book already written, and the Lord brought me again to the themes of Psalm 20, which in many ways summarize the heart of David's leadership expressed in all his psalms. Through this process, the Lord overwhelmingly affirmed His power as I prayed the themes of Psalm 20, and He gave me a monument to share with Christian business leaders who seek *Business after God's Heart*.

Praying for Leadership

Psalm 20 is a prayer for the people of Israel to pray for King David—and remember it was written by David. This psalm is David's divinely inspired exhortation and guide for those under his authority to pray for him as he led Israel. Praying for those in leadership is a consistent theme of scripture and the Spirit leads David to be specific and direct in his exhortation to the people of God to pray for him as he led.

Throughout my career I have prayed for those in authority over me. I picked up the habit while a new believer at the Naval Academy during my earliest Bible studies and through the ministry of more mature Christian navy officers. The application was made to 1 Timothy 2:1–3 where Paul exhorts Timothy to pray "for kings and all who are in authority." So in the navy I prayed for the president, the secretary of defense, the admirals in my chain of command, the captain of my ship, and my department head—all with increasing granularity as I became closer to those I interacted with daily and felt the impact of their judgments, those who had huge influence on my life. On the quarterdeck of my ship, that's the ship's formal entryway from shore, was a large wooden board with pictures of everyone in my chain of command, from the president of the United States down to the captain of my ship. This visual aid became part of my habit of prayer each day, and I continued to pray in this way after I left the navy and entered the business world.

When I prayed, I lifted up my boss and my boss's boss every day. I believe the Lord has used this, shaping my heart to serve and support those in authority over me with sincerity, in obedience to God, and this sincere attitude has paved the way for great relationships with mutual trust and success.

David's Inspired Prayer

The same Spirit who inspired Paul to tell Timothy (and us) to pray for those in authority over our lives in 1 Timothy 2 also inspired David to give this specific prayer in Psalm 20 for the people of Israel to pray for him as he led them. In chapter 7, "Leading with Humility and Confidence," we saw in Psalm 8 that "[He] made us a little lower than God … to rule over the works of [God's] hands" and that He put all creation under our dominion. This work that God delegated to man is accomplished through business. So as business leaders, we are on mission from God to subdue the earth. God has given us authority and power for this mission.

So let's consider this prayer in Psalm 20 from "the heart after God's heart" as not only David's prayer for his leadership of Israel but also as a prayer for *your* business leadership. In our meditation to apply God's Word to our hearts, let's think of Psalm 20 as David's prayer for you. Since we know this psalm is "living and active" (Hebrews 4:12), let's ask the Spirit to bring it to life at the depths of your soul.

Praying for Your Leadership

Applying this prayer to you and your leadership in business will change your heart, elevate your focus to God's perspective on day-to-day challenges in your business, and help you embrace your identity through Christ. It helps remove your subconscious tendency to separate your business life from your devotional life as it helps you recognize your work is God's work; it is holy and for His purposes.

Prayer for Faith (Like Sight) in Daily Trials

> May the LORD answer you in the day of trouble!
> May the name of the God of Jacob set you securely on
> high! (Psalm 20:1)

If you call your business challenges, problems, troubles, or issues "trials," then you will see that the everyday flow of business involves trials (as we discussed in chapter 6, "Business Trials"). And by the sheer weight of time, most of your trials in life are business trials. So as you pray about your business day, pray for the Lord's answers and support directly related to the troubles of today. Look for His answers today. Have faith that He will answer. As you order your day and prepare for your meetings, pray that God will guide as you plan and know that He will answer on point when you engage your issues/problems/challenges. Pray with confidence that He will provide in the little trials for the day and the bigger trials that seem to continue for many days and months as well as those that may seem oppressive. As you pray, in the same way you expect to have trials, also expect that the Lord will "answer" entirely enough for today, as you walk with Him.

In your prayer, envision God's active engagement as you ask Him to "set [you] securely on high (verse 1)!" "Securely on high" is another picture of the Zone of your heart, recalling from chapter 6 this place David also refers to as "under His wings," a "rock," a "fortress," a "refuge," a "tower," and a "shield." So while you pray that God sets you securely on high, you engage your faith with your imagination to "see" that He has indeed set you securely on high and that He is your Rock of stability and strength as you lead, a Fortress of protection, and this secure high place is His Tower from which He provides visibility of business threats not yet known.

One Thing (Again)

> May He send you help from the sanctuary
> And support you from Zion! (Psalm 20:2)

David then leads you to a focus in prayer for God to "send you help from the sanctuary." Your mental image as you pray may drift to one that has you praying to your Lord as if He is outside you. In fact, we know that the sanctuary of the presence of the God of the universe is within our hearts. So you're praying for help from the One who is more than just very near, as we saw from David in Psalm 139 and chapter 4 ("God in Your Business Thoughts"). He is within each of your thoughts and even before each thought, as your heart begins to form thoughts, you know your help is so powerfully near that your prayer for help is being answered as it is formed with Him in your mind. What an amazing gift for your soul and what a powerful, confident place for your heart to dwell as you engage in the day's business. Remember David prayed for one thing. "One thing I have asked from the LORD, that I shall seek: That I may dwell in the house of the LORD all the days of my life, to behold the beauty of the LORD And to meditate in His temple" (Psalm 27:4). God answered so abundantly for us through Christ, and as you consciously dwell there, in His presence by His grace, you are certain that He will send you help from that sanctuary of His presence in your thoughts.

So Much Better than Burnt Offerings

> May He remember your meal offerings
> And find your burnt offerings acceptable! (Psalm 20:3)

As you pray the themes of this prayer over the perplexities and challenges you face in your business, you may be aware of sin in your life or in your area of business responsibility. This sin hinders your embrace of God's presence in your thoughts to send you His help in your business trials. No doubt David felt this too. We addressed this extensively in chapter 2 as we looked at David's great prayer of confession and repentance in Psalm 51. And now as you pray authoritatively with David, you are reminded that you can't look past unconfessed sin in your life. David didn't. We see in Psalm 20:3 that he made a "burnt offering" for his sin. While he prayed that God would find that offering "acceptable," as you confess your sin, know for certain that the sacrifice of Christ is so supernaturally "acceptable" that God sees you with Christ's perfect righteousness. How totally liberating it is to proceed in business from this position of purity and spiritual power! All because of God's grace and mercy poured out on you through Christ as you lead in your business.

No Wimpy Prayers

> May He grant you your heart's desire
> And fulfill all your counsel! (Psalm 20:4)

When I pray the themes of Psalm 20 for my business leadership, I realize how many wimpy prayers I've prayed. Here David prays, "May He grant you your heart's desire and fulfill all your counsel!" As we reflect again on the extremely high view and calling the Spirit through David affirms about us in Psalm 8, you recall that you're almost a star-maker! God is in constant contact in your thoughts and is ready to answer as you seek His support for this big job. Maintain this perspective of being on God's mission as you exercise dominion over the earth through the daily details of your work and pray that He gives you the right counsel and the right desires *and* that He fulfills those counsels and desires.

Jesus picks up David's theme of confidence in prayers for those walking with Him as He said in John 15:7–8, "If you abide in Me and My words abide in you, ask whatever you wish, and it will be done for you. My Father is glorified by this, that you bear much fruit, and so prove to be My disciples." As you abide in Christ while leading your business, you should pray with confidence that "He grant you your heart's desire and fulfill all your counsel!" (Psalm 20:4). It is a very confident heart that prays that prayer with integrity and humility, and that's part of a heart after God's heart. This heart does not pray wimpy prayers!

Praising God for Victories Not Yet Won

> We will sing for joy over your victory,
> And in the name of our God we will set up our banners.
> May the LORD fulfill your petitions. (Psalm 20:5)

The heart after God's heart sings God's praises for all He is, all He has done, and all He is doing—as we addressed "The Business of Praising God" in the last chapter. Here in Psalm 20, David leads us to praise God for success (victory) that has not yet happened. Praising God for success in business, when that success has not yet happened, demonstrates enormous faith and dependence on God for business. Really getting your heart there—to praise God for success that hasn't yet happened—shows who you're really trusting. Praising God for outcomes that haven't happened changes your heart. When Psalm 20 was prayed, David was on his way out to war with his army. He was actively engaged with all his gifts and abilities, and men and equipment, but his exhortation was to praise God for victory that had not happened. Ahead of him was still the battle and he would not just lie down and praise, but he and his people would give praise for victory that would come about through God as he engaged with his army.

Take a moment and think about a real challenge (trial) that you face in business. Now really and truly praise God for His victory in that situation, knowing He might take the long or indirect way that brings more glory to Him. Now *stop*. Praise Him more for that success that hasn't happened yet. He's got this! *Stop* again. Praise Him for that solution He hasn't yet given. He is sovereign and very active in your heart and your business. *Stop*. Give Him sincere praise for victory not yet seen. The great God of the universe who loves you infinitely and unconditionally *is engaged!* Praise Him! We can praise Him for solutions, successes, and victories not yet given because we are certain He works *all things together for good* for those who love Him (Romans 8:28). This substantively puts your heart at rest in your business trial (challenge, issue, situation, problem). Your staff needs to be led through a difficulty (trial) by a leader whose heart is at rest, not fretting or anxious. This helps set everyone at ease and increases their focus and capacity for greater effectiveness.

Praying for God's Saving Strength

> Now I know the LORD saves His anointed;
> He will answer him from His holy heaven
> With the saving strength of His right hand. (Psalm 20:6)

Now David's prayer gets very deep and prophetic. We know David was the Lord's anointed and a type of Christ. Throughout the psalms, the Spirit inspired him to prophetically speak the words of Christ. In chapter 3, "The Broken Business Leader," we saw David prophetically identified with the crucifixion of Christ, speaking Christ's words from the cross. We know the Lord saves King David, His anointed leader of the nation of Israel, called for God's purposes. We know that Christ, "in the days of His flesh, He offered up both prayers and supplications with loud crying and tears to the One able to save Him from death, and He was heard because of His piety" (Hebrews 5:7). And God not only saved Him through His resurrection, but He also glorified Him. Through His sacrifice on our behalf, we know that God saves us. So we are really wrapped up with David and with Jesus in this amazing prophetic prayer.

Your work in business is God's work and as you lead there, you too trust "in the saving strength of His right hand." God's strength that saved you from hell through Christ is the same amazing strength you trust in now as you pray *this prayer* inside the challenges (trials) of the business God has given you to lead. You pray in faith for God's saving strength to engage your heart as you touch your business. God's saving strength is the strength of reversals; it's the strength for the dependent; it's the strength for the poor in spirit; it's the strength in brokenness. It is a power engaged in your life "from His holy heaven," where came the great works of the God in creation, in resurrection, and where Christ is now exercising His exalted power to prepare an eternal home for you.

Seeing all this, you pray for His saving strength to touch your business problems (trials) and He begins to shape your heart and your business perspective as He did King David's. God answers these prayers with the power that is His. "The saving strength of His right hand" is clearly not referring to mystical thoughts or weak desires built on nothing but the cravings of our flesh. We pray to the God of the universe, and He is fully engaged with infinite power and divine sovereignty. The God of all creation is physically engaged in the business you lead for His divine purposes!

You're driven by your faith in God's saving strength to redeem each moment as He is active in the tiny details of your thoughts and everything you touch (or that touches you). Having done His work of salvation, your Lord remains just as powerfully and redemptively engaged in the details of every business day and with your every business thought. Pray accordingly!

Clear-Minded about the Real Cause of Our Success

> Some boast in chariots and some in horses,
> But we will boast in the name of the LORD, our God.
> (Psalm 20:7)

The core message from the flow of the prayer in Psalm 20 is contained in verse 7. "Some boast in chariots and some in horses, but we will boast in the name of the LORD, our God." And in some ways this message summarizes everything that the heart of David has for the leader who wants to lead a business after God's heart. David's words here combine an expression of faith with praise, all reflecting a heart of dependence on the Lord. We need business plans, program plans, capital, processes, sales, recruiting, and all the rest. David had all the implements of war and had to do the business of governing, leading, and winning with strategies, tactics, and these implements of war. In fact, this prayer was prayed on the occasions of his departures with his army to engage his leadership gifts, his fighting men, and his military equipment in war.

When you are honestly trusting in the Lord during your business troubles (trials), so much so that your heart is "boasting" in Him amid those troubles, you are centered, at peace, and even full of joy. You have the implements of business that you seek to apply effectively as God has gifted you, just as David still had the implements of battle, but the engagement of your business skills and resources come from a heart/psyche that is actively boasting and praising the unseen Lord your God with all power in heaven and on earth.

Never Again Trust in Chariots

During my agonizing business trial referred to at the beginning of this chapter, in my extreme despair as I led what seemed to be a hopelessly failing company, the Lord brought me to these themes from Psalm 20. "May the LORD answer [me] in the day of trouble [today]! May the name of the God of Jacob set [me] securely on high! May He send [me] help from the sanctuary and support [me] from Zion!" God also helped me recognize that over the years I've felt at times I had great business strategies and tactics yet still failed, and other times felt I had far less business means yet was successful. And the Lord very practically brought my heart to the certainty that it's not about my chariots or horses. It's all about that one thing that David sought: to consciously dwell in the presence of the Lord, relying on Him completely.

Do Not Let Your Heart Be Troubled

David's prayer in the day of trouble recorded in Psalm 20 is paralleled by the words of Jesus to His disciples (and to us) in John 14:1–2 as He exhorts us, "Do not let your heart be troubled." Then He tells us what to do instead. "Believe in God, believe also in Me. In My Father's house are many dwelling places; if it were not so, I would have told you; for I go to prepare a place for you." Jesus said to me in my business trouble, "Bill, do not let your heart be troubled." His exhortation was not to allow my heart to be driven by business troubles. Instead, I needed to consciously put my faith in action: faith in all He is, all He has done, all He is currently doing, and all I will experience together in the eternal dwelling place that He is preparing for me. My heart can't be troubled while consciously believing all this about Him in the moment. And He really did become the boast of my heart, setting aside all the "chariots" that I had been trusting. Instead, I focused on the certainty of His amazing work, past and future, and for His direct engagement in my heart now with infinite, unconditional and eternal love and sovereign power amid my business troubles.

As I prayed, the Lord answered me from the sanctuary of His presence in my heart and in my active thoughts to set my heart at ease. I had peace and was able to function effectively in the real confidence of God's active engagement for His glory in my business troubles. And while I still didn't know how He would work out the practical business issues, His victory had already happened. After that remarkable moment, my heart was settled; I was sleeping well and had peace and joy in my faith as I continued to lead.

A "Monument" to Share

Less than a month after this very poignant experience with the Lord, a vice president walked into my office to tell me we just won a contract that was bid several years prior. This was before I joined the company so I asked about the size of the contract. He didn't know immediately because all the arrangements were made before he joined as well. Later, he checked with our legal team, and they determined that our contract value was $150 million! We celebrated together for a few minutes, and I set out to discover exactly what we had just won. Within a week the same vice president walked in my office to tell me we had won another contract, the business arrangement likewise made years prior, and that the value of the contract was $50 million. And amazingly, the next week, he walked in *again* to inform me of yet another win of another $150 million contract. All this happened inside two weeks on business arrangements that were made years prior to the engagement of current staff and only attributable to the movement of the hand of God. This represented a total of $350 million in new business for my $90 million company! These things just don't happen. In fact, my senior staff came to refer to this event as "manna from heaven!" To which I heartily agreed! Nobody had ever seen or even heard of anything like this.

This was a total game-changer. And I knew that it was a clear sign from God that had less to do with the business than it had to do with my heart of trust. The victory was not in the business reversal but in the work of God in my heart, and He created this physical monument in business to demonstrate His powerful direct engagement and unmistakably confirm His work in my heart. I also knew that God created this "monument" not only for my own faith but also to share as an encouragement with others.

Ending with This Prayer for You

> Save O Lord;
> May the King answer us in the day we call. (Psalm 20:9)

David ends this prayer similar to the way he began in verse 1. And we end our study of the of the heart of David applied to your heart in business like we began: praying with David from Psalm 20:1 that "the LORD [will] answer you in the day of trouble! May the name of the God of Jacob set you securely on high! May He send you help from the sanctuary and support you from Zion!" As God does indeed send you help from the sanctuary of His presence amid your thoughts, and at the depth of your soul, I pray God will produce in you a heart after His own heart and through your heart will emerge a *Business after God's Heart.*

Printed in the United States
by Baker & Taylor Publisher Services